A Place Called

A Memoir

By Sharon Grace Smith

This story is inspired by true events. Some names and identifying details have been changed.

To help our environment, 5% of profits from sales of this book will be donated to One Tree Planted. To learn more about this charity, please visit onetreeplanted.org.

Cover design by janetatwork.

Printed in the United States of America
ISBN: 9798986792507
Library of Congress Control Number: 2022915282

For Mom

*Happy is the house
that shelters a friend.*

– Ralph Waldo Emerson

Contents

Risk

Dear Michelle,

I am determined to get this letter off to you in the morning mail. Marci and I have been in and out all week every chance we could find, collecting newspapers for band expenses. Some of our collecting was fun as we talked to neighbors along the way who have been saving papers for her all summer. And some of the collecting was just plain hard work. Marci just spent the entire school in-service day off on Friday, I kid you not, stuffing newspapers in bags and organizing them in the station wagon for the first run to the high school.

I got up early on Saturday morning and collected from a few more people who had been saving papers for her. The band members dropped by the parking lot all morning where their individual stacks of papers were measured. Marci ended up with 40'9" of papers at 50¢ a foot, making her goal of $20. What a project! To think she plans to keep this up all year. Help!

While on one of our trips collecting, I saw a big old house near our friend Barbara's place. It was old, yes— but kind of inviting. She said that a FOR RENT sign had just been placed in the yard the day before. Evidently, the owner no longer lives in town, and the word on the street is that it's hard to find good people to rent houses these days. I'm thinking about checking it out, as it's close to the high school, a requirement for us, but probably too expensive. More on this later.

So, tell me, how is the apartment? I heard that your dad came over with the table and chairs from our kitchen. Isn't it funny how that darn table just does not want to leave our family? Yours is the third place it's been, to my knowledge. We divided the lamps, end tables, some pictures and dishes. I was happy you could use the kitchen set.

I've been expecting that you would feel a little lost and alone the first couple of days, no longer living on campus. How are you doing? I know I felt lost when I was your age and on my own the first time out of the nest, so to speak. The hard part is no phone. Yikes! At least you now have silence to concentrate on completing your studies. If we need to, we can make quick calls from work and school for now.

Please find the enclosed money to help you grocery shop, etc. I can't wait to have a proper visit. The mailman is due to arrive at any moment now, so back to work I go.

Love you more than tongue can tell,
Mom

And So It Begins

I KNEW I PROBABLY COULDN'T AFFORD IT, but curiosity got the best of me. On impulse, I drove to the house, swung into the driveway, and put the car in park.

In the middle of the huge yard, a young man sat high up on the seat of an old riding lawn mower. Mesmerized, I sat in my car for a while just watching him ride back and forth across the lawn. Then, as I looked around, I noticed a garage set farther back at the end of the driveway. The doors were open, and a bedroom dresser and a bunch of boxes were piled up in front. There was no vehicle in the garage and none on the property or even parked in front of the house.

I hesitated for a minute more, wondering if I should bother flagging down the lawn-mower guy.

Finally, I got out of the car and yelled, "Hey!" as loud as I could, waving my arms around.

He stopped, jumped down, and walked toward the car. His hair was tied up and in a long blond braid down his back. His jeans were worn, and he looked at home in his faded Guns N' Roses t-shirt. "Yes, ma'am?" he replied as he reached me.

"Do you know anything about the FOR RENT sign?" I asked.

"Yes, ma'am, I do. I have a number right here." He pulled a tattered piece of paper out of his pocket and handed it to me. "It's the owner."

"Do you live here?" I asked.

He smiled, "Yes, I do...or *did*, but I'm movin' out now." He smiled again, his face lighting up. "I sure enjoyed living here. The house is real nice, real big. And it's got a great yard with all these trees."

He spoke quickly and kept looking to each side of the driveway and up and down the street. I wasn't sure if he was anxious to get back to mowing or if he was just nervous talking to me. Just to understand him, I had to watch every move or gesture he made and concentrate carefully on his speech, as his words seemed to tumble out of his mouth.

He seemed to know a lot about the house, the property, and the whole area. He explained that the house was well known by several of the old-timers living in the area since it was around when they were growing up.

He turned slightly, spreading his arms wide and pointing with his dirt-stained fingers toward the street saying, "I heard there used to be large old trees lining both sides of the street. Their leaves reached over. Made kind of a tunnel underneath." He looked down at his sandals and said sadly, "One after the other, they were cut down."

"I would've loved to have seen them," I replied. "I'm sure they were beautiful." My words seemed to satisfy the young man—he was now relaxed and smiling again. I thanked him for his time, and as I backed out of the driveway, I felt a stirring of unexpected excitement.

Truth be told, I felt nervous, too—probably because I was about to close on the sale of our family home and had been feeling apprehensive yet hopeful about my next step. Being recently divorced after twenty years of marriage, I'd have to learn to live without a partner. I hoped to find just the right place for myself and my daughters. We needed a place within walking distance to the school. A place where we could begin anew. A place to call home. Maybe this house was the answer.

I lived in many houses while growing up. My parents divorced when I was twelve years old. My older sister, Annette, had already left to be on her own when my mother, her new husband, and I moved out of Seattle and into a nearby rural area. That was my first exposure to living outside the city, and it was a real shock to me. I attended a school that required me to ride a big yellow school bus with lots of noisy kids. At the time, I thought those buses were a real letdown. I was accustomed to walking to school and then, later, riding to school in sleek city buses, quiet and cool.

Getting comfortable living out in the middle of nowhere, as I thought it was, took several months for this city girl. I wasn't used to seeing cows in pastures, farm equipment parked in fields or beside roads, and large houses on huge pieces of property. In the city, houses were often pressed up tight side by side with very little space between them. Before this move I'd seen very few homes with big lawns. In time, though, my mother helped me learn to enjoy the adventure of moving out of the city. We often took drives to find nearby shorelines. She and I both loved to sit near the water, smell the salty air, and watch the boats go by—all of which became regular parts of our new life in the rural Pacific Northwest.

We ended up moving around a lot, which was difficult for me in some ways, but perhaps this experience of getting used to new surroundings as a child helped prepare me for the experiences that would unfold later in my life. Accepting the things I couldn't change and learning to make the most of the experiences in front of me was a valuable lesson—one that I was destined to repeat many times throughout my life.

As young adults, my husband and I lived in Claremont, a charming town located in a valley just outside Seattle. The buildings in town were rarely more than two stories high. When our first child, Michelle, was five years old, we moved to a residential neighborhood just south of the downtown core. Shortly thereafter, our second daughter, Marci, was born. The girls spent their childhood in that friendly suburban neighborhood.

When I registered Michelle for school, I was introduced to the principal. He asked if I was willing to volunteer when needed for school activities and events. With a desire to do my part, I heartily agreed. He went on to say, "Make sure your children's teachers know you. Help them whenever they ask." He told me that if a parent was involved in their children's school, the kids would get a better education. Taking his advice to heart, I soon became actively involved with teachers, parents, and children.

During those early years raising the girls, I spent many hours creating and sewing costumes for Michelle's dance classes and events. With new acquaintances, I went to many lectures on health and parenting, where I asked many questions about how to handle dietary issues for little Marci (who we discovered had numerous food allergies). I'm not sure how I managed all the activities I was involved in, but in those days, from what I assumed, this was all part of being a "Super Mom."

Several years later, I began working part time at a local insurance company's streetside office in the center of town—an area full of small-town charm and amenities. Comfortable benches just outside the building offered people a chance to rest, reflect upon the day, or wait for friends. And nearby picnic tables provided a perfect spot for lunch breaks during the warmer months. The area also featured a small but versatile staging area where the town committees conducted meetings, local talent entertained, and aspiring politicians spoke about what they could do for their constituents. In early spring, the city hung up wood planters, which would soon be bursting with colorful flowers and plants— geraniums, petunias, alyssum, creeping Charlie, and sweet-potato vines cascading over the rims. Throughout the summer, local artists displayed their sculptures here and there. And during every season, colorful flags provided by the local businesses flew from both sides of the main street in the center of town. All these decorative touches enhanced the already spectacular views of the mountains situated on both sides of the valley.

For many years we were a happy family in a lovely community. But over time, I began to realize that my husband and I were drifting apart, becoming distant in every way. Our marriage was very good until it wasn't.

Our divorce was painful not only for us but for everyone in our family. From that point forward, everything in our lives shifted. We were no longer going to be in a home all together as a budding family or have a lovely yard that little children played in for hours. We would no longer be in a place with wonderful neighbors who we had known for many years. We would no longer look out our windows and recognize the dogs, the cats, and the mailman who drove by daily.

My husband and I had started out our life together at the age of eighteen, so young and full of "can do" spirit. Now I was about to find out whether I could handle the "can do" part of life all on my own. I wondered whether my mother had felt the same all those years ago when she'd divorced. Once my life settled down a bit, I would make a point of asking her. For now, though, I was very aware that I had two beautiful girls to finish parenting, and I needed to move forward as well.

One evening as I lay cuddled up in bed, preparing to go to sleep, I began to feel quite strange. My chest started to feel heavy, and my heart seemed to beat loudly. My mind raced with ominous possibilities: Was I having a heart attack? A stroke? Whatever it was, I didn't have time for this! My body couldn't do this to me! How could I afford to take care of myself and my two children all on my own? I began to pray fervently for direction, and fortunately, my body began to relax.

After that experience, I spent many nights lying in bed talking to God about my fear, asking for help to overcome its power. I would breathe in slow, deliberate breaths and repeat—over and over—"Let go and let God. I am not alone. I am loved. I am worthy. I can do this." As I did this more and more, I began to settle down and feel a release of mental confusion and bodily fatigue. In time, a quote came to me that I remembered reading in a book somewhere long ago:

*All glory comes from
daring to begin.*
— Eugene F. Ware

But was I ready to begin again? Would I be able to laugh, love, and live happily again?

At this time, Michelle was away at college, but Marci was still in high school. So the challenge would be for me to find an affordable home near her school and my workplace. Leaving our familiar residential setting was going to take a leap of faith. I'd have to find just the right place. But would finding such a place be possible in the downtown corridor of the city we had come to love so much?

Marci and I spent time talking about what was important to us. We both wanted to live in town but knew that the chances were probably slim. Housing was in short supply. My sweet mother lived nearby and was aware that we needed to find a place. She knew some people who lived in the area, so she shared our hope with them. Within days, one of her friends called to tell her about a house with a FOR RENT sign in the front yard. She said the house was on a large lot in the middle of downtown Claremont on a street with just a few other smaller houses on each side. And most importantly, it was within blocks of the high school.

Through a little research of my own, I discovered that the house had been built in the early 1900s and had over 3,000 square feet of living space. My mind swirled with the possibilities of things we could do there. What an adventure living there might be for us. Yet one daunting question lingered in my mind: how could a newly divorced woman with limited funds, one child in college, and one in high school ever afford such a charming old place? The house would probably be much too big to manage and much too expensive to rent. Nevertheless, after work I drove by the house to take a look.

There was a covered porch across the front of the house. A framed wood and beveled glass door with large windows on either side was set in the middle. Six steps led down to a walkway with boxwood bushes planted on each side that extended to the main sidewalk. The bushes were a little out of control and needed pruning, but the entry to the house had the potential to be quite appealing. I visualized pots of flowers hanging from the front porch providing an inviting sense of peace and harmony. With the landlord's phone number in my pocket and a bit of encouragement from the fast-talking guy on the lawn mower, I decided then and there to take a risk. I would call that very evening.

14

Mr. Van was an absentee owner looking for a renter he could trust to take care of his house as if it were their own. He and his family had moved out of the area several years earlier. I told him my name, phone number, where I worked, where I used to live, and what I was looking for—including my desired budget. I was relieved when he assured me that he was willing to negotiate the rental price to have the sort of renter he wanted. Some repairs were in order, but he suggested I take a tour of the house and then call him to discuss specifics. He couldn't be there in person but would make sure I had a key. I called my mom and asked her to come walk through the house with me the following day. Despite my concerns about the size and price of this house, I couldn't wait to see the inside.

Finally, the next morning arrived. Sunshine poured through the trees, casting beams of light through the branches. As I walked toward the car, the most beautiful butterfly greeted me. "Good morning," I said to the butterfly when it landed on the hood of my car. It fanned its wings for a while before taking flight, having accomplished its mission of greeting. We were both ready to set forth into the day.

That afternoon, Mom and I drove over to the house, where a prearranged key was waiting for us under a rock near the front door. I was again feeling that sense of excitement, like we were on a mission to discover what the future would hold.

We stepped inside to a generously sized living room, which spanned the full width of the front of the house. At the right end of the room was a fireplace with a bookcase on either side. The fireplace had a wood mantle painted white with a mirror just above and a beautiful iron grate across the front hearth. The bookcases were situated below leaded glass windows, which provided some nice light coming into the area.

As I stood looking at the fireplace, I sensed a cozy library area. The damp and drizzly months of the Pacific Northwest were always the best time to snuggle around a warm fire with a good book. Later when I learned we couldn't use this fireplace because it had been damaged by an earthquake, I was saddened. Nevertheless, in the year to follow, this hearth would indeed prove to be a hospitable gathering space for our blended family.

I noticed that the windows across the front of the house, which faced southwest, continued around to the side of the living room, where there was another very large window. In the afternoon, it was like standing in a pool of sunlight—so warm and inviting. I also noticed that those big, beautiful windows were missing drapes. If we ended up renting this house,

I'd have to find some before winter set in to keep the cold out.

To the left of the living room was the main hallway, which led to a shower room, then to the main bathroom, and then to the master bedroom and bath. If you exited the living room to the right, you entered the dining room, where we discovered a wall of windows. Beneath the windows was a padded bench with an open grille, which we thought might be a cold-air return. It was full of what appeared to be bird droppings, seeds, and feathers. What a mess! The former renter obviously had birds.

The wall that separated the dining room from the kitchen had a built-in china cabinet with drawers and shelving. One of the drawers had green velvet fabric fitted around the inside with separator slats for the silverware. Surprisingly, after all these years, the leaded glass doors on the cabinets were in great condition. My mom commented, "The set of china and serving bowls I gave you years ago would sure look pretty in that cabinet."

"They sure would," I said. The missus of this house had probably enjoyed entertaining in this room with her good dishes and silver nearby. I would love to have the opportunity to do the same. This would be such a lovely room for building family memories again. With a smile, I visualized a table with damask linen tablecloth and napkins.

The living room, dining room, and hallway all had good hardwood floors—scuffed and dirty but certainly not too bad considering the age of the house. Mom suggested that they simply needed some love and attention.

As we continued our tour, we found ourselves in a huge farmhouse-style kitchen. This kitchen was obviously built for someone who liked to spend time preparing food for a lot of people. More windows across the back wall above the sink and counter overlooked a massive backyard. Just to the right was a breakfast room separated by another built-in cabinet. Between the upper and lower cabinets was a traditional pass-through. The breakfast room also had more windows all around as well as a door that opened to the side yard.

In the hallway and going halfway up the stairs was a large landing with a tall, beautifully encased double window facing northeast, which would be an advantage for letting the sun in during the early morning hours. I loved the amount of light in this house. For a dark time in my life, the light would be a welcome guest.

At the top of the stairs to the right and left were narrow doors that accessed storage areas tucked under the eaves of the house. The second floor included a half bath plus three large bedrooms, each with its own large closet. We discovered that the basement level also had two bedrooms as well as a separate part that was mysteriously covered in dirt. In some areas, the floor was buried under a foot or more of dirt while in other areas you could see bare cement poking through. How odd, I thought.

A fairly new oversized electrical panel hung sideways, barely attached to the side of a wall. What was this all about? Why the dirt? Why the electrical panel? We would have to ask the owner some questions about this. Did he know about the mess? Clearing it out would take a bit of work, but Mom and I agreed that once this part of the basement was back to normal, it would make a great storage area.

The laundry facilities faced the backyard. After what we'd just seen with the piles of dirt and all, I wasn't expecting much of this room, but thankfully, it was nice and clean. Off to the south side of the basement was a small room that looked like it might have been built to store canned goods. Empty shelves lined the walls. Mom and I visualized these shelves filled with veggies, fruit, pickles, meat, and beans. When I was a child, most homes had storage areas like this. Families would gather in the fall to make their favorite canned delicacies. Ours were end-of-the-garden relish, old-fashioned chow-chow, bread-and-butter pickles, and of course Mom's favorite, pickled beets. We also found the old fuse box for the house, which had us both questioning why there was an additional electrical panel in the other part of the basement.

Going out the back door, we saw plum and apple trees growing in the yard. "Oh, they'll be beautiful in bloom come next spring," Mom said. Beyond these trees, the yard stretched so far back with foliage that we couldn't see to the edge of the property. To the side of the house was the garage, which was large enough to hold a car and a work area. It was empty except for the riding lawn mower. A small pile of used lumber was stacked just beside the door.

A touch of love makes all things
well again.
— Author Unknown

What a lovely old house. It looked like it could be quite grand as it stood on this large lot. It needed a good cleaning, yes, and some repairs too. I also had some questions about the dirt we'd found. I had a few suspicions. Working at an insurance office, I was aware of properties being misused. I wondered whether the owner knew what had been going on here. Often, absentee owners are not aware of problems that come up. They're usually informed by a friendly neighbor or city officials or when the rental payments cease. Whatever happened there, I may never know. But happily, the owner decided it was time for a change.

Mom and I had been making a list of all the repairs we could clearly see needed to be done. Being a longtime homeowner myself, I was relieved knowing that those repair projects would not be my responsibility this time around. I would be a good renter for him and planned to ask him about repairs that needed to be done.

During my life, whenever I've been alone or afraid, I've always felt that there were angel guides assigned to help me. While I'm not sure where I got this idea, feeling this way has always seemed normal to me. I have a strong belief in a power greater than myself. I often call on my guides, talk through my worries, ask for help, and listen for guidance.

The night before our walk-through, I had a strong vision of us living in that big old house. I didn't share this with Marci right then. Later, as my mom and I sat down for tea (as we so often did), I shared with her my vision and what was going on in my mind. Maybe my idea was a bit out there. Still, I said to her, "Why not consider a home where Marci and I could live and share the expense with others?"

Many years ago, I had an experience of sharing the expense of living in a large and stately old home. I lived in another city right after I graduated from high school. Two elderly gentlemen and I lived in a home where a widow boarded out her spare rooms for extra money. She made the evening meal and provided laundry facilities for us. I worked in a department store nearby and walked to work. This was in a town near a military base where my future husband was stationed. We were married not too long after that, but my stay in that home was a pleasant one. Why couldn't we do something similar here? My mother, always supportive of my ideas, said, "It surely has possibilities."

I continued, "I bet other people are going through big changes in their lives. Maybe they need a place to stay for a while. I enjoy helping people, and now I need help too." What would work for me might just work for someone else as well. A shared expense, hmm...

The Project

THAT EVENING AFTER DINNER, I told Marci about the house, sharing my enthusiasm about the house itself as well as its convenient location: only a few minutes by car to my workplace and a ten-minute walk to her school, which would make it easier for her to participate in musical activities and other school events. Then, with a bit of trepidation, I told her about my vision for sharing the house with boarders.

I needn't have worried about her reaction, though—when I asked how she felt about living with strangers, she immediately said it sounded like fun. She even suggested that the two of us should interview potential housemates together. I thought this was a great idea and proposed that we share our thoughts and feelings with each other about everything unfolding from this point on.

We started by creating some house rules:

- No men allowed upstairs.
- No overly loud music or other noise.
- No alcohol and/or other drugs on the premises.
- No overnight guests.
- No long-distance calls without permission.
- We will provide a shower and clothes-washing schedule.
- We will provide simple breakfast options; you're on your own for lunch.
- Dinner is at 6:30 p.m. during the week; Friday night you're on your own.
- Saturday and Sunday dinner, you may join in if you're home.

Since I planned to prepare dinner every night anyway, I was happy to cook for my housemates as well. That big kitchen was made for preparing family meals. I had lots of dishes, pots, and pans and looked forward to the possibility of sharing meals. Besides, I could try out some of our family favorites on others and tweak a few of the recipes in the process. I loved the idea of having a sit-down dinner where we could touch base with one another at the end of the day, a tradition I enjoyed very much during my married life while raising our children.

I lay in bed that night, my eyes pressed closed, my mind wide open. I mentally cleaned and decorated the house over and over, positioning books, plants, pillows, curtains, tablecloths, and vases here and there. Simultaneously excited and exhausted, I finally fell asleep.

When I woke up the next day, I felt a calmness of spirit. I realized that a power greater than me was in charge here. I knew I was being supported. My belief that we would prevail led me forward. I was not alone.

I called the owner, Mr. Van, first thing that morning. After some discussion, we agreed on a price and a schedule: Marci and I would move in the following month, which was only a few weeks away. He offered to compensate me for cleaning the inside and making it move-in ready. I gladly accepted, although I knew there was a lot of cleaning to be done. I explained to him what my mother and I had discovered on our walk-through: the electrical panel hanging off the wall, the dirt covering the basement floor, the many broken or cracked windows, the leaky faucets in the bathrooms, and the filthy cold-air return in the dining room. We decided to start by calling an electrician to take care of the panel hanging off the wall in the basement. (We held our breath, hoping all was still electrically safe within the home!) After that, Mr. Van would come out and take care of all the other repairs in a timely fashion.

Before our conversation, he'd known there were problems but hadn't known exactly what they were. He just knew that the house hadn't been well looked after for some time. He'd stopped receiving rent and had heard from several neighbors that people would come and go quite often. The city had contacted him about what seemed to be an abandoned car parked in front of the house. So he seemed happy to have found a responsible renter to take care of his investment.

When driving by the house on my way to work that day, it appeared empty. No cars, no people, no boxes or furniture in the yard or driveway. Yay! The renter had moved on. And suddenly, we were moving forward.

The next day, I walked over to the office of the local paper and placed an ad: "Room for Rent." I felt in my heart that this was what I needed to do. I knew that the right people would show up for us.

While I was at work, my mother's friend Barbara called and offered to help us clean the house. I was so encouraged by her friendship, love, and support. I decided to get started that very afternoon.

After work, I cleaned the main bathroom, shower room, and the master bath. Barbara stopped by with a stack of barely used white lace curtains that she'd collected over the years of moving from one house to another. They were the exact length to fit the dining room windows and would look beautiful hanging there. The unexpected fit of these curtains was one of the many little miracles we would experience in this house.

Over the next few days, my mother, Marci, Barbara, and I swept and washed the floors. We ironed and hung up the lace curtains. Barbara even managed to transform the cold-air-return grille in the window seat—under all that filth was a gleaming gold brass grate. Between that and the new bulbs we put in the chandelier, the dining room came to life and was ready for any occasion. Simply beautiful! And within a week, the whole house had taken a turn for the better.

The following Saturday morning, I met with the electrician. He walked around the basement and poked his head into the little canning room where the main circuitry panel was located for the entire house. He came out, smiled at me, and said, "Now *this* was quite the operation!" In response to my confused look, he explained that the basement had clearly been the site of a "private garden." Evidently, the lumber I'd seen piled up by the garage had been used in the basement to hold grow lights, and the pile of dirt suddenly made sense.

As the electrician tore out the useless wiring and updated the electrical panel, he shook his head. "The previous tenant obviously had some, but not a lot of knowledge of electrical wiring. He could have started a fire, switching wires around the way he did. He sure got lucky."

And so had the house. It had survived the operation, and the era of growing plants in the basement was now over. From now on, its only job would be to house very grateful tenants.

Several days later, on the way home from work, I felt compelled to swing by my favorite secondhand store. My intuition was rewarded when I found a stack of drapes sitting on a table just inside the front door. Apparently, they were recently donated by a couple who had cleaned out a large home in town. They needed washing and a little work on a new hemline, but other than that, they were exactly what we needed for the windows in the living room, rods included. Another happy miracle! My mother and Barbara could not believe my luck. For me, this was confirmation that my personal guides were indeed hovering above me, helping out.

Over the next few days, we continued our cleaning to get the house move-in ready. Barbara's husband arrived with his handy drill and ladder. He carefully climbed up the ladder with Barbara holding the sides while I handed him the rods one at a time. Soon they were installed over each window in the living room. I had recently spent several evenings cutting and hemming the drapes and curtains to fit. When we were done hanging them, we felt we'd made great progress toward our moving-day goal.

I called around and organized a moving party for the following Saturday. Friends were so gracious and willing to help. With the extra hands, I hoped we'd be able to get everything moved in one day.

When the big day arrived, Barbara's husband picked up the moving truck and brought it to the house bright and early. Amazingly, we were moved out of our house in the suburbs and moved into the big old house in downtown Claremont by late afternoon. We sat around eating pizza, drinking iced tea, laughing, and giving each other a hard time about how we would never apply to work for Smoother Movers, our hometown moving company. One day was hard enough. Who would do this full time?

As I'd thought during our walk-through, the area by the living-room fireplace with the beautiful built-in bookcases did become our library and reading area. There we placed a straight-backed chair and rocking chair along with a magazine rack and side tables with nice reading lamps. All this made for a lovely area, as I'd envisioned. At the other end of the expansive living room, we created a TV-viewing or conversation area with a couch covered in pillows and, nearby, an old love seat draped with a cozy afghan. We also had a couple of older recliner-type chairs that, eventually, we'd all fight over when getting ready to watch movies together.

Our move-in day went well, but I felt a mixture of emotions: plenty of excitement, a little fear, and also some sadness. I was saying goodbye to the past and welcoming a new tomorrow. I went back to our family home and cleaned it up for the new owners to arrive the next day. Driving away, I said some prayers for them, including "Godspeed" and then, for myself, "God, please help me accept this change with grace and dignity." While I was grieving one chapter of my life being over, I was overcome by a sense of gratitude for a new beginning. Thankfully, I had found a place for us to call home.

When I look back on those early days, I'm amazed at how certain I was that this move was the right one. Moving into a house that obviously needed repairs was one thing, but inviting complete strangers to come and live with us was quite another. Yet I never thought for a moment that this vision of mine might be a mistake. Perhaps having the confidence of previously being a homeowner and the good memories of living in that boarding house just after high school were giving me the inspiration needed for this adventure.

> *It's not how much we give but how much love we put into giving.*
> *— Mother Teresa*

Around the time of this move, I remembered this quote by Mother Teresa. I knew that I was about to love the heck out of that house and all who would come to live in it! And I knew that I was about to experience a different kind of community, living with and giving to people whom I had never met before.

Dear Annette,

Thank you for the beautiful card and letter of encouragement. It came at just the right time, as does the message in it: Risk, Receive, Rejoice! I love it. Sisters are the best!

We've finally closed on the house. That was really tough for me, even though I knew it had to be. Just as soon as we had a buyer, however, I got busy thinking about where to go. I mentally put our needs out there and began visualizing our next most perfect home. I made a list and just went over and over it. Quite suddenly, a possible answer arrived.

Mom and I discovered a house for rent in the middle of town and not far from the school. It's a big old house, but I now have a big idea—a vision of sorts. My plan is to rent out some of the rooms like a boarding house. This shared expense will help me cover the rent, groceries, etc. and maybe provide help to others who need a place to settle as well.

I fluctuate between feeling super confident (I can do this!) and then feeling quite terrified. What have I gotten us into? Yikes! I really am on my own. This is a risk for sure.

I will do my best to keep you up to date on our "Project," as Marci and I refer to our plan.

Love you more than tongue can tell,

Sharon

Housemates Arrive

E VA DISCOVERED ME through a mutual friend. She too had recently gone through a divorce and was starting over on her own. After moving from California to Washington, she had just interviewed for a bookkeeping position in a local furniture store and was looking for a place to stay while figuring out what to do next in her life. As I spoke with her by phone, I was surprised at how quickly we fell into a comfortable conversation. I sensed that we could enjoy each other's company. We agreed to meet after work the next day.

As I was trying to go to sleep that night, I wondered whether Eva had been sent by one of my hovering angels. They were surely aware that I needed someone to come live with us. For this experiment to work, I needed help paying the rent.

But sent so soon? We had just moved in the week before.

Eva arrived the next evening—a cheerful, petite, thirty-five-year-old brunette with beautiful glacial blue eyes. I immediately noticed her sparkling energy and the bounce in her step as she greeted me with a lovely plant, a purple African violet. What a sweet and thoughtful thing for her to do. It was the first of many African violets that would find a home on our kitchen window ledge, the perfect spot for them to receive the morning sunshine they love so much.

While I freshened up after work, Marci gave Eva a tour of the property and the house, including the upstairs room that would be Eva's. The room, located next to Marci's, had a double bed, an old but nice chest of drawers, a desk with a lamp, and a chair. The room faced south, which meant that a lot of light poured in from the windows, even in the late afternoon. Eva loved the size and feel of the room as well as the big closet with lots of shelf space.

As I prepared dinner, I heard them talking and giggling. A wave of joy washed over me. Perhaps this was our new beginning.

I invited Eva to stay for dinner so we could continue getting to know each other. During our meal, I discovered that she was very accomplished in many areas of her life, including her career, and that she had a grown son who lived in California. When I asked her what she liked to do for fun, she told me she loved to read mysteries, go to movies, and play board games with friends. Then her eyes sparkled and she added, "I also have a bit of a sweet tooth and love to bake. But most of all, I love to dance. My son does too. He's in a group that performs routines for entertainment at parties and such."

While saying our goodbyes after the enjoyable dinner together, Marci promised Eva that she'd research and ask her friends for a few new board game ideas. And once we were alone again, Marci told me that she felt good energy from Eva and that in her opinion, she'd make a good housemate. I trusted my daughter's instincts and agreed with her assessment.

Happily, Eva called the following day with the news that she'd gotten the job as the furniture store's bookkeeper, so she'd definitely be staying in the area and would love to live with us. I was excited for her and for us. We agreed on the shared expense, and she agreed to the house rules. Her plan was to move in the following weekend.

I felt blessed that Eva had found us so quickly through a mutual friend, and in the excitement of her agreeing to stay with us, I'd forgotten all about the month-long classified ad I'd placed. So I was surprised when a few days later I got a call from Margaret, a woman who lived in Seattle but was looking for a place to stay during the week. She told me she worked at a college near us and wanted to avoid the long commute, which she found simply exhausting on a day-to-day basis. Her plan was to return to her home in the city for the weekends.

We met the very next day, and I quickly felt she was a perfect fit for us as well. She had a warm smile and came directly to the point. She liked where we were located, agreed to our house rules, and could afford to pay her part of the expenses. Marci wasn't home from school yet, but I was sure she'd like Margaret too, so I took a chance on the spot and agreed to have her stay with us.

A smile is a gift
you can give every day.
– George Elliston

Over the course of Margaret's stay with us, we saw very little of her. We would hear her leave very early every weekday morning when she'd slip away to swim at the local YMCA, come back to change her clothes, and then speed off to begin her day of teaching. She often came in after dinner and went straight to her room. Several months passed before Marci and I felt that we were beginning to know much about her at all.

Eventually, I learned that we did have some personal circumstances in common. Margaret was also divorced and had raised a daughter on her own who was now happily married and living in the Seattle area. Marci and I enjoyed Margaret's personality and looked forward to spending more time with her whenever she came home early enough to have a little visit with us. However, we were always aware of her desire for quiet and privacy.

As time passed, we learned that Margaret loved receiving massages, facials, manicures, and pedicures. She would often tell us of her latest treatment or show off her newly painted fingers and toes. This woman sure knew how to pamper herself and did so with great enthusiasm. At that time in my life, I'd never taken personal time for myself. I was just too busy taking care of others around me, or so I told myself. But with Margaret staying with us, my understanding of self-care changed. I realized how important personal time could be. Because of Margaret, I had my first professional pedicure, and to this day, I set aside time for personal care.

The four of us soon settled in nicely together. But although I was grateful for Eva and Margaret, I began thinking that we really needed another housemate to share the expenses. And just like that, my thoughts were heard. An answer came through loud and clear the very next day.

Jacob answered our ad in the paper with a phone call asking if a room was still available. To my surprise, I said yes without much thought. I don't know why, but I had not considered that a man might call. I told him we could meet and talk about the possibility. Then I immediately wondered, What was I thinking?

That evening we four women had a little talk about having a man in the house. Would we feel okay with that, would we feel safe? Our answers, we decided, would depend on the person. Even though I'd already agreed to the meeting, Marci and I were still a little nervous to meet with our first potential male housemate. We knew we needed to have some trust, so I decided to just let go and let his story unfold.

Jacob was a clean-cut, average-sized forty-year-old with permanently tan, leathery skin from working outdoors for most of his life. We quickly discovered that he was a displaced logger from the southwest part of our state. He was a polite, likable guy, but a little on the shy side. He seemed a bit nervous too—understandably, as we asked lots of questions and expected answers to every one.

Jacob told us, "My wife, Sara, and I live in a small trailer at an RV Park on River Road. I'm not working steady right now, and we're getting on each other's nerves. We need some separate space for a while—temporarily, I hope."

As Marci and I listened with open hearts, he continued, "I receive some compensation, but I don't have a lot of money."

I was concerned about whether he could even afford to pay us a full shared expense, but there was something about his sincerity and seeming honesty that attracted me. Something in my gut told me to show him the room available. I later learned that neither Marci nor I felt a sense of unease while spending time with Jacob. Maybe it was the fact that he had been a logger, which may seem silly to some people, but in my years growing up here in the Pacific Northwest, I had a very good impression of his profession—good, hard-working men who felled our trees and brought valuable wood to the market. Logging was a respectable job back then. I remember as a child, my mother and father had several friends who worked in the logging industry.

On the way back up from the downstairs bedrooms, Jacob noticed the dirt on the main part of the basement floor and casually commented on how many wheelbarrow loads he thought it would take to remove it all. As Marci showed him around the property, she asked, "Do you know how to use a riding lawn mower?"

With a smile, he said, "I'm sure I could handle it."

That answer was very nice to hear, as it occurred to me that we were going to need someone to help us with outdoor maintenance. As we sat around the breakfast room table, we talked about meals, to which he responded, "Oh, I actually don't eat a lot." I was taken aback by that, as I had been wondering whether we would have enough food to satisfy him. Loggers were known to have huge appetites.

I asked him about the house rules, and he thought that would be fine. We talked about the year-round outdoor maintenance. He agreed on a partial shared expense and would be willing to work in exchange for the rest.

Marci and I looked at each other and then at Jacob. Taking a deep breath, we agreed to take yet another risk. He was a stranger yet seemingly very sweet. He had a lot to offer us. Meanwhile, Jacob would have a place to stay while he sorted out his life. We now had only one room left.

Shortly after Jacob moved into the house, he began scooping up the dirt in the basement. I could hear his shovel dragging against the cement off and on for several days. I was amazed. He had guessed correctly. Exactly forty wheelbarrows full of dirt were pulled out of there.

Days later, I pulled into the driveway to see the garage doors wide open. Jacob was bent over the riding lawn mower. He decided it needed a good going over and had cleaned and oiled it. It was ready to go, and so was he. Before long, Jacob was sitting proudly atop the old mower, happily buzzing around the yard—a splendid sight!

Soon, it was time to contact Mr. Van with an update on the care of his home. We hadn't talked since the electrician had been here for repairs. I had previously sent him a list of everything in need of repair that Mom and I had observed on our walk-through. I wanted to give him a little good news. We now had a clean floor in the basement—no dirt!— and a reconditioned lawn mower, both thanks to Jacob. I felt a sense of satisfaction in sharing that information with Mr. Van.

None of us, including Jacob, would have known then that living with us would be the very catalyst that began Jacob's journey toward a brand-new way of life—one that he never expected to experience.

One afternoon, I was relieving the gal who worked at the front desk at work when an older gentleman popped into the office. He introduced himself as Jack Daniels and said he was there to see his friend, agent Will Jones. While waiting for Mr. Jones to be available, he struck up a conversation with me. I must say, not only was this man friendly and lighthearted, but he was also very entertaining. He immediately launched into a story that "only you could appreciate," or so he said. I would later learn that this was the shtick he used on everyone! His story included hand gestures and small vocal noises and ended with a hearty laugh. He reminded me of a character out of a vaudeville show.

Later that day, Mr. Jones asked to see me in his office. I headed down the hallway to meet him, a little curious as to the purpose of our meeting. As I walked into his office, Mr. Jones looked up. "Sharon, have you ever met Jack Daniels before?"

With a smile and a barely restrained giggle, I said, "No, not until today have I had the pleasure and surprise!"

Now both of us were laughing, his head nodding knowingly. "Jack is quite the character. As it happens, he's in trouble right now and needs a few friends to help him out. His wife of many years has asked him to get out of her sight, her life, and their home. He is, as you would imagine, quite upset. He claims he has no place to go and can't afford to completely relocate. As a longtime friend, he hoped I might have an instant solution to his problem."

Still unsure why he was telling me all this, I wondered if he had somehow found out what was going on in my personal life. I hadn't had the chance to tell him about our "project."

Mr. Jones continued, "You and I have lived in this town quite a while, so I thought I would ask if you would talk to a few people. Hopefully, someone you know could take him in until things settle down a bit between them."

I asked Mr. Jones if he wouldn't mind first giving me a little background on Mr. Daniels. If I was to help at all, I would need to know a little more about him.

He smiled and said, "Please sit down; this might take a while, as I've known him for many years." And so we talked about Jack for some time.

He told me that he'd been Jack's insurance agent and friend through the ups and downs of life, that Jack and his wife were originally from California, and that their children were now raised and no longer living in town. Despite his wife's demands, Jack didn't want to be too far away from her, as he was sure she would need him, given that they both were in their late seventies.

He also shared that Jack had been in show business for many years. "Back when Vaudeville was popular, before silent movies became the thing, Jack was a fairly well-known manager of several large theaters in L.A., Chicago, and New York City. He claimed to have been tight with some of the greats."

In those days, large theaters had built-in pipe organs, large stages, and lots of seating. When entertainers, musicians, and comedians on the traveling circuit would come to town, Jack would often introduce the acts. This is where he got his ability to draw people into his world.

Mr. Jones continued, "At that time, Jack rubbed shoulders with all sorts of characters—circus acts, singers, comedians. Of course, comedians were his favorite. There was a lot of socializing that went along with his profession, and he enjoyed every minute of it. As I got to know him over the years, he'd tell me how there'd be more meetings and interaction with entertainers, more dinners, and more drinks."

I found all this rather interesting, especially because my father had been in sales for a theatrical supply company that supplied goods to theater-owners up and down the coast of Washington and Oregon. Being in sales meant that my father often traveled to meet and entertain customers. Sometimes sales calls would last until late in the evening with many rounds of drinks. I remember hearing my mother talking to my dad late at night about him entertaining customers where the drinks flowed, the nights became mornings, and his ability to function became questionable.

I learned that Jack had spent a lot of his life on the road and wasn't around much as his children grew up. He thought he could make up for all the time away from his family once he was retired. Instead, he discovered that his family didn't wait for his retirement. The children grew up and moved on with their lives. Now he had a son in California, a daughter in Oregon, and a wife asking him to get out of her life.

Did we want to take on someone like Jack Daniels, even temporarily? Would he fit in with the rest of us? He had a lot of energy, and I wasn't sure if he was someone we could handle. But I could clearly see that he needed help, even if just for a short time. Despite my reservations, I felt sorry for Jack and his wife. Maybe because of my parents' struggles so long ago, or perhaps because of my own divorce, I had an increased empathy for others going through marital strife.

After talking all this over with Marci, we decided to meet with Jack. When I got to work the next morning, I spoke with Mr. Jones and quickly explained my current living situation. "We do have a room available in our house, but Marci and I first need to interview Jack. We need to get to know him a little more and see if he'll fit into our mix of people there before having him live with us."

As he leaned back in his chair, Mr. Jones smiled and said, "Good for you and for Marci too. A great idea." Mr. Jones had always been a cheerleader for the girls, and I trusted him. He continued, "Jack is a good man with a big personality. He has high energy and a big heart. And he's quite an entertainer, so sit back and enjoy the show."

I called Jack that very day and told him I might be able to help him out. I invited him to meet with us Saturday afternoon. He heartily accepted.

When Saturday afternoon came, Marci and I were standing in the living room looking out the window while expecting his arrival. He turned into the driveway and slowly inched his car forward, taking a few minutes to get parallel to the porch. Finally, opening his door, he got out with flowers in one hand and what looked like a large blue book in the other. As I saw him stand up and turn around, I thought he must have been quite tall in his youth. Now, despite being a little hunched over, he was nevertheless quite a handsome elder in his red plaid shirt and khaki pants. He cautiously climbed up the front steps with the book tucked under his arm so he could hold the flowers too, then with his other hand, he reached for the railing.

I opened the door and greeted him with a smile. He stood proudly before me, paused, bowed slightly, and handed me the bouquet of flowers, saying, "The flowers are for you, madame."

Aww, what a charming guy! I showed him to the dining room where I had set out some tea and cookies. He and Marci immediately started chatting and, not surprisingly, got along very well—so much so that I could have gone grocery shopping and left them on their own!

I asked him to share a little of what he was looking for in a living situation, to which he responded frankly, "I need very little—just a place for a very short period of time. I wish I could stay at home, but that's not an option right now."

I explained our intention, vision, and rules for the house and then said, "Jack, even if you're going through a tough transition, there ought to be a place where you feel safe. There ought to be a home where you can feel a sense of family." And then we offered him a room.

He looked down at the table as he accepted our offer, assuring us that the arrangement would only be very temporary. After all, he wanted to go home as soon as possible. I invited him to join us for dinner that evening, and he looked up with an expression of pure delight.

About this time, Jacob came in the back door and up the steps into the kitchen. When he popped his head into the dining room to say hello, I introduced him to the newest member of our family community. Jacob pleasantly and respectfully welcomed him. I could tell he was a bit curious about this new man with whom he'd be sharing the downstairs area. Even though there was quite a difference in age, I felt they would soon be quite comfortable with each other.

Jack promised to return in several hours for dinner after going home to tell his wife where she could soon find him. As he said his farewells, I could see that while he was not thrilled to be leaving his wife and home, he was really happy and even a bit excited that he had a place he could call home for the time being.

That evening, after Jack returned and dinner was ready, we all gathered in the breakfast room just off the kitchen. The only one missing was Margaret who, as usual, was away for the weekend. I introduced Eva to Jack, and she loved him right away. They easily fell into a comfortable banter.

Sitting there all together, I mentioned that Marci and I had been saying the Serenity Prayer before dinner every night for some time now. I suggested that we could continue the tradition together if all agreed. Jacob was the only person at the table who didn't know the prayer, but Jack had a copy of it inside his book sitting nearby.

Within a few days, Jacob had the prayer down by heart. Everyone thought that saying this prayer was a great way to come together for dinner each night. We would take turns starting it, and then everyone else would join in. For our first dinner together, I began, "God, grant me the serenity to accept the things I cannot change, the courage to change the things I can, and the wisdom to know the difference." I felt strangely comforted by their voices—Jack's deep and sonorous, Jacob's quiet, and Eva's chipper—along with me and Marci in unison.

We had a lively and deeply connecting dinner together that evening, the first of many sitting around the table in that quaint breakfast room. One by one, each of us shared how grateful we were for the roof over our heads, the food for our needed nourishment, and the opportunity to be part of a community of friends living together as family during this time.

After dinner, we each said goodbye to Jack. He planned to begin his stay with us in one week. I watched as he slowly and carefully backed out of the driveway to the street. I never did get used to watching Jack drive. He was agonizingly slow behind the wheel. I was grateful he was being careful, but I imagined that it took patience to be driving behind him.

I soon learned that Jack loved to be in the kitchen. He enjoyed cooking his specialties. I would discover that he had a few surprises up his sleeve.

How beautiful a day can be
when kindness touches it.

— *Author Unknown*

Touching Base

MARCI AND I WOULD OFTEN END OUR DAY by touching base with each other. We sat propped up on her bed with pillows all around us and talked about our day and the plans for our tomorrows. We were feeling encouraged that everyone in our home seemed happy to be here. We now had a full house, we mused, sighing happily. Thank you to the Universe and my angels above for all the help.

Now we needed to concentrate on the future. Marci had exams coming up on her agenda and more college-application forms to fill out. She had a goal: she wanted to get as much financial help as possible through scholarships to attend college. Being five years younger than her sister, she'd watched Michelle struggle financially to afford college.

The divorce had had a huge impact on Michelle. Our savings for her college education were depleted, and there weren't many scholarships available at the time. She did get some help through financial aid and also worked steadily throughout her college years, but it was a challenge for her to manage.

Because Marci saw this, she wanted to be as organized and ready as possible. She set up banker's boxes and created her own makeshift personal filing cabinet filled with folders holding applications to individual colleges, copies of community services and activities, and booklets she had requested from colleges she was considering. She was as determined as she was organized!

The next few months were going to be very busy for her and really important for her future. Her goal was to receive a full scholarship and make sure her college expenses would be covered.

Like my daughters, I also grappled with financial uncertainty. Divorce had been painful and confusing in many ways for me. And although I was haunted by grief over what might have been, the fear of poverty was far more pressing. Struggles surrounding money after a marriage ends can be overwhelming. I didn't see many women raising their children on their own, let alone being the sole breadwinners for their family. Instead, I saw many single moms living in poverty, their children with grandparents or in foster care. Fortunately, sharing expenses helped provide some breathing room and gave me a little extra time to think about what was next for us.

Now, looking back on my life, I believe that, like many women of my generation, I'd been groomed to be a wife and homemaker. Financial security played a big part in that way of life. I never considered college, nor was it talked about. I never thought I would be forced to get by completely on my own.

As I cuddled next to Marci, I realized I was feeling a sense of relief for the first time in years. And as I felt more comfortable, I began to embrace living with and learning from the people around me. Angels, friends, and strangers were beginning to show me how to find my way.

Dear Michelle,

We have a full house. Can you believe it? Marci and I have met, interviewed, and are now housemates with Jacob and Jack (downstairs) and Eva and Margaret (upstairs with Marci). We've had some enlightening conversations around the dinner table in the evening. I wish you were here now to meet and greet all these lovely people. You would enjoy them. We have created quite a family community in this house.

I'm relieved and grateful to share the expense, which makes this all possible. I remind myself not to get into worry and fear around how long it will last. So I'll take this one day at a time and appreciate the gifts I receive.

Mom comes over for tea and dinner quite often. You know how great a friend and confidante she can be. She is "Mom" to some and "G-ma" to all. Everyone loves her as if she were their own. And you wouldn't be surprised to hear that she is also making herself known as quite the pie lady. Next time you're here, we'll put in a special request for blackberry pie, your favorite.

Love you more than tongue can tell,

Mom

P.S. Money enclosed for shopping.

Receive

Falling Leaves

BEAUTIFUL LEAVES WERE FALLING all around the yard. As the weather rapidly changed, so did our way of living. We no longer aired out the house with doors or windows wide open. We began to leave galoshes by the back door just in case they were needed, and just inside we began to use the wall hooks for holding our coats and jackets. We hung hand towels to wipe down whatever came in through the back door: packages, groceries, and such. And I noticed that we became hungry for more soups, stews, pot roasts, gravy, and roasted vegetables.

One Saturday morning, the doorbell rang at eight o'clock. I was just waking up, not even out of bed yet, so I let it ring. But a few moments later, it rang again, followed by a loud knocking, then banging on the front door.

Okay, okay! I got up, threw on a bathrobe, and headed down the hallway. Through the front door's glass panels, I saw two police officers and a lady standing on the front porch.

Perplexed, I opened the door and asked, "What's going on?"

One of the officers replied with a question in return: "Does Jack Daniels live at this address?"

"Yes, he does," I answered, "Why?"

The other officer handed me a couple of documents: one that gave them legal authority to be here and the other, a list of things that Blanche, Jack's wife, claimed he had taken from their home without permission. The officers and the counselor were there to retrieve those personal items. I invited the three of them to come inside. As they stood by the door, I headed for Jack's room, feeling pretty fuzzy-headed and wondering how this was all going to work out.

I knocked on Jack's door. Not a sound. I knocked harder. He swung the door open yelling, "What, what?" I explained that two police officers and a woman were here to see him. He had fallen asleep reading his blue book, which now lay beside his bed on the floor. He quickly put a bathrobe on over his pajamas and came up the stairs behind me. "What is this all about?" he asked.

Not wanting to be the bearer of this news, I said, "I'm not really sure; let's just let the officers explain."

The officers introduced themselves and the counselor. "We have authorization here to search your belongings. If you have anything listed on this document, we are to retrieve the same and return it to the family home."

Jack responded respectfully to the officers and counselor, but his voice began to inch up louder and louder. He looked at the list of things he was accused of taking. "My wife is mistaken! I'll show you everything I have. You can come to my room and see for yourself." He grew increasingly frustrated and dramatic, waving his arms around, which caused his bathrobe to fall open, untied. Fortunately, he was adequately covered by his pajamas. Raising his arms over his head, he said passionately, in his loudest stage voice, "She's out of her mind! She's out of control! I went quietly, as she requested, and took nothing that wasn't mine." He was just barely in control of himself.

Everyone in the house was wide awake by now. Peeking down the stairwell, the girls could see Jack, two uniformed officers, and the unknown woman standing in the hallway. Jacob was in the breakfast room drinking coffee as they paraded by the kitchen door, following Jack down the stairs.

I quickly went into my room and got dressed before going to the kitchen. Soon after, Marci and Eva came downstairs in their bathrobes and joined us. Margaret had left late last night for the weekend and missed out on all the commotion. Not quite knowing what to make of all that had just happened, the four of us just sat at the table saying nothing. We drank our coffee and tea and looked at each other, waiting for the household to return to our normal Saturday morning.

After the officers and counselor left, Jack stood in the middle of the kitchen and, with an air of defense, said to no one in particular, "They found nothing that was on that list." I imagined he felt embarrassed for being part of such a scene after only having been with us a short time. He apologized profusely and disappeared into his room.

I'm well aware that we all have a past. We've all experienced awkward situations or simply had uncomfortable relationships at some point. Certainly, my past has included raised voices, misunderstandings, and times when communication completely ceased. Still, this morning's wake-up call had been disconcerting for everyone.

By that afternoon, though, the house had settled down again. Marci was studying in the breakfast room. I sensed she needed to be close to me. Eva was resting in her room. The guys were hiding somewhere in the house or yard. Normally, we were all gone or involved in our own personal lives and therefore not home or not interested in a sit-down dinner on a Saturday night. But this weekend started off unnerving for everyone, and we welcomed a chance to come together to share a peaceful meal.

I was happy to make dinner for our family; cooking was a nice way for me to calm myself down after the unexpected events of the morning. When dinner was ready, I called everyone to the table.

Jack again apologized for disrupting our Saturday morning and offered to entertain us as a thank-you for the inconvenience. "How about we meet in the living room after we tidy up the kitchen?" he said.

The day that had started out so abruptly ended with music and laughter. Jack had a routine where he would play his violin beautifully for a bit and then abruptly stop to tell one of his little stories and a joke or two, often a one-liner that was corny but oh-so-funny. He reminded me of Jack Benny, a popular old-time comedian and talented violinist.

We all laughed and listened and ended our day with love and a feeling of home in our hearts. Tears filled my eyes as I reflected on how, after such a short time together, we were a community of souls learning about kindness and family unity.

It was another Saturday, and I was standing in the hallway just outside my bedroom door. I paused and assessed the activities of everyone in the house. I could see that Jacob had just started a jigsaw puzzle on the card table in the living room. Jack was fussing over a pot on the stove. Standing near the kitchen sink, Eva was making morning coffee. I could hear Marci in her room upstairs practicing her trombone for the school's winter concert. Smiling to myself and feeling very happy, I offered silent thanks for the blessings of having housemates. I realized that I was growing increasingly confident, too, trusting my instincts, and letting my inner voice guide me. I was so much happier than ever before. A wonderful new me was beginning to emerge.

That afternoon, as I was cleaning up the kitchen, I overheard Marci visiting with Jacob in the breakfast room. He was telling her about a job that he had to quit even though it was his first after many years of logging. He worked for a company that taught him how to repair fax machines, the latest mode of communication. Unfortunately for Jacob, it turned out to be a dead-end job. He was on the road a lot and realized he wouldn't make enough money to live on, let alone support a wife. Jacob was trying to make the change he knew was necessary now that employment in the logging industry was no longer sustainable. He was feeling undereducated with only a high school diploma and no other usable skills. He was depressed.

Marci couldn't just sit there and listen to Jacob sound so discouraged. She got up and walked over to the kitchen sink, sighing and staring out the window into the backyard as she filled a glass full of water. I knew that Marci wanted to help, but how? I wondered how she would convince Jacob that life wasn't over for him.

She walked back to the breakfast room and sat directly across from him. Looking straight into his eyes, she said, "Stop it! Just stop it, Jacob!" She leaned forward, putting her hands on the table. "Okay, things haven't worked out for you yet. So, start over. You're a hard worker, and you are smart; you could succeed at whatever you decide to do. Start by talking to a counselor about possible jobs. Ask questions. Find out if going back to school would help you."

Jacob looked up at her with a blank stare and just sat there, seemingly immobilized. Perhaps this was all too much for him. After a few minutes, he began lamenting again that it was just too late for him. He was just too old. He wouldn't fit in anywhere. "What company would ever hire me?" He got up quickly and went out the side door to the yard.

Marci looked over at me and just smiled. Even at her young age, she was like an old soul, gifted. She knew that patience was really important with Jacob and that education would free him from despair. We both really hoped Jacob would realize this someday soon. Knowing Marci, she wouldn't let the matter drop.

*Most of the shadows of this life
are caused by standing in one's
own sunshine.*
— *Ralph Waldo Emerson*

After living together for a while, we fell into a routine where we all gathered together for dinner, especially during the early part of the week. On Friday and Saturday nights, however, we often went in different directions. Marci and I had previously agreed that Friday would be a "you're on your own" night. On Sundays, I would always prepare a big family dinner. If people were home, they were welcome to join us.

Friends would often ask me why I was fixing dinner for people with whom I shared my home. I thought, Why not? Over the years, I'd perfected several delicious, hearty soups. I love casseroles and became known in the neighborhood for my savory gravy and sauces. I enjoyed making meals that made others happy, and I took pride in my efforts. I soon found out I wasn't the only one who felt this way.

From the very beginning of Jack's stay with us, he would generously offer to make a meal or two. This was so kind of him, but I was a little worried about letting Jack loose in the kitchen. Unsure of what to expect from this senior, I would profusely thank him and then go ahead and make dinner anyway. I hoped that my loving gratitude for his offer would be enough to satisfy him.

It wasn't.

Soon he would offer again. He finally wore me down with his incessant offerings. I could clearly see that he really enjoyed being in the kitchen, so I threw caution to the wind and decided to give him a chance. The first thing he did when he got into the kitchen was to wave a big spoon in the air and chase everyone out.

It turns out, my concerns were unwarranted—his meals were delicious! He specialized in dishes from "his Italy." Lasagna was his favorite, but we also looked forward to his spaghetti with homemade meatballs and fragrant sauce. (We all agreed he could make a mean sauce!) He would proudly serve us his form of love, and our family community thoroughly enjoyed his personal recipes and the stories that went with them. And eventually, I was even allowed to watch him create a few of his magnificent entrées.

While Jack wowed us with his Italian delicacies, Jacob made good on his promise to care for the yard.

Throughout the fall, we grew familiar with the sight of him sitting high on the riding lawn mower, buzzing around the yard. He was amazing! He was able to do the whole yard—front, side, and back—within a couple of hours, including way back under all the trees. With the changing season, though, he mowed less and raked more. The yard was filled with poplar, maple, walnut, and several varieties of fruit trees, and as their leaves fell, Jacob raked them up and stacked them into huge piles. The mix of colors was beautiful.

One Saturday morning while Eva, Marci, Jacob, and I were sitting around the breakfast table, visiting and having a second cup of coffee, I looked out the window and commented that the huge pile of leaves reminded me of my childhood. In my neighborhood, my friends and I would meet up and race around from yard to yard looking for the biggest mounds. When we found a good one, we'd look around for any adults who might stop us, and if the coast was clear, we'd take a running start and jump right in.

Jacob grinned as the four of us looked across the table at one another and then outside. As one, we stood up and headed out the side door. With yelps, hoots, and hollers, we all became little kids again, jumping up and down, chasing one another in and out of and all around the piles. Jack had followed us out the door and stood to one side, waving his arms, laughing, and eventually supervising us as we calmed down and helped Jacob rake the leaves back up again. Even as we raked, we kept laughing, and we all agreed that being a kid once in a while was great.

The flowers in the hanging baskets and pots on the front porch were just about done blooming now. The time had come for us to change the look of our entrance to a fall setting. Growing up in suburban America, it was normal to see the changing seasons reflected on the porch or entrance of neighborhood homes. Many paths and porches would be decorated for whatever holiday would soon be celebrated. This year we decided to decorate with baskets of some of our colorful leaves from the side yard. Of course, with Halloween coming up next on the calendar, we would include a few pumpkins and squashes. Maybe some corn stalks and brooms too.

First, choosing a few pumpkins was essential, which meant that it was time for something I always looked forward to: our annual sojourn to one of the huge pumpkin patches in the valley fields nearby. Marci and I picked up Mom on a Saturday morning, and off we went. We had a fine day for the trip, and driving there was half the fun. We followed the country road as it meandered over a train track, around a bend in the road, and across a bridge over a river, passing farms, strawberry fields, fruit stands, and interesting old farmhouses.

When we finally arrived, we watched the owners busily directing people to rows of variously sized pumpkins so that buyers—often families with little children—could pick out what they wanted. This farm sold many varieties of squash. They also had several stands set aside containing jars of home-canned pickles, veggies, fruit, and more.

The farmer and his wife greeted us with a wave. Mom waved back. "Good to see you!" she said as she reached for a few jars of their pickles and beets, of which she was very fond. To the side of the checkout table were three-pound coffee cans full of dahlias wrapped in brown paper and string, their purple, yellow, red, and magenta heads peeking out above the paper cones.

We brought home pumpkins, squash, beets, pickles, corn, and bouquets of flowers for Mom and me. Over cups of tea, we inspected our purchases and considered how to arrange them on the front porch.

Later that afternoon, we grabbed the baskets from our collection stored in the garage and dove right into our project, arranging the baskets of leaves, corn, and other props on the porch and steps. When we stepped back to admire our work, we felt ready for fall. Also, we were now ready for our neighbors' children to visit on Halloween night.

At dinner, Eva complimented us on our decorating skills. "I plan to be home on Halloween night," she said cheerfully. "I love seeing everyone all dressed up. May I answer the door? Do you mind if I dress up too?"

I said, "I think that would be wonderful."

She continued, "I have a witch's outfit I'd love to wear." We were all delighted by the idea of that. Perhaps we would all dress up.

I said, "I'll be the old woman who lived in a shoe." We all laughed.

Jacob grinned. "How 'bout I be the Tin Man."

"Great! And I'll be a big black cat," said Marci.

Jack announced that he'd be a clown. He also offered to pick up the candy the next time he was at the store. We thanked him in advance for the candy, and we all agreed that he'd make a perfect clown.

"Sounds like we have a good plan," I said.

Then Eva asked, "Do you think the weather will hold up and be clear that night?"

"Well, I've been listening to the radio," Jacob said. "The weather report for Halloween is fair, no rain."

And the forecast proved to be correct: it was a perfect night for trick-or-treaters, and we had plenty! The doorbell rang almost constantly all night long.

Every time we opened the door, we'd see a new batch of kids: little kids with their parents, big kids with their friends, and everyone dressed up, laughing, and having fun—including us! Each of us had the opportunity to show off our costumes many times, and our visitors seemed to enjoy our enthusiastic participation.

We all went to bed happy that night, the little kid inside us perfectly satisfied.

Love is perfect kindness.
— Joseph Campbell

One evening, Eva asked to see me in her room after dinner.

Over the past few months, we had become pretty close. We seldom discussed big issues—such as our past marriages or what had or hadn't happened as we'd hoped—but we did share many details of our daily lives: the books we'd been reading, the great items we'd picked up on sale, where Eva had gone dancing on the weekend, and who she'd met. We really enjoyed our visits and would sometimes meet after work on Fridays, have dinner out, and catch up on details of our week. But until then, I hadn't entered her room (or any other rooms, simply out of respect), so I was curious about what she wanted to speak to me about.

On my way up the stairs, I wondered what she'd done with her room to make it her own. It didn't take me long to find out: the moment I walked into her room, I looked around and thought, This is so Eva. It was light and colorful, and every detail seemed to embody her warm, cozy style: the afghan on her bed, the fabric thrown over the rocking chairs, the mini prep table for her tea, and even the cups and plates she used for the tea and cookies she'd prepared for us that evening. Everything was so pretty. I took in a deep breath and felt that I had actually inhaled the peacefulness of the setting.

Sinking down into her big old rocker facing me, Eva shared that she'd gone to an appointment with a new doctor who had discovered a lump in her breast. She was worried but also hopeful. She asked if I'd accompany her to a follow-up appointment next week with a specialist who would test for breast cancer.

Of course I said yes.

Worry and Fear

THE RESULTS came back positive.

I was so glad to be there supporting her as a friend—when she got the results and also for the weeks and months ahead. She would not go through the ordeal of surgery and radiation alone. I knew that Eva would try to stay positive, and so would all of us in the house. Once she got the dates for the procedure, we as a family could make plans as to how to help at home. Her doctor advised her to continue working and not to worry. Easy to say, hard to do for us all.

Propped up in bed that night, I thought about how alone and scared Eva might be feeling. It reminded me of all the days I stayed home alone as a young girl. I had infectious mononucleosis, and the doctors decided that I should be homeschooled, so I spent most of my sixth-grade year at home. Every Thursday afternoon, Mrs. Alton from the school district would come to teach me math, history, and English. But most of the week, I was by myself.

My mother and father both worked, and my older sister, Annette, was off to school early. Mom would set out lunch for me and remind me that she'd call on her break. When Annette arrived home in the early afternoon, we'd have a snack and catch up on what we'd done that day. She would share with me who she'd seen and what she'd learned in her classes. There were times when she'd stay home to take care of me. I'm sure that missing school on these days wasn't easy for her, which made me feel guilty.

I was scared sometimes, too, worried about how long I would be sick and what would happen to me. But I often listened to classical music, which helped soothe my fears. Our father played two instruments: bassoon and saxophone. He loved all music but was especially fond of the classics. Around the time I was sick, he bought a fairly large, beautiful piece of equipment for the family: a mahogany record player that was so big that it looked more like furniture than stereo equipment. My father accumulated many classical recordings that I probably listened to more than anyone else in the family.

I remember the first time I lifted the top and peered inside at the turntable, which accommodated the size of records of the day: 78s.

Dad taught me the proper way to play the records, carefully removing them from their sleeves and gently placing them one at a time on the turntable so I could listen during the day when I was alone. He also taught me to clean the records with a special cloth and how to carefully return them to their sleeve.

While everyone was gone, I pretended to be a radio announcer, making up creative monologues announcing to my listeners what they were about to hear. I didn't pay much attention to the records' titles or composers. Many were actually difficult to read, or I didn't know how to pronounce them. I sat on the floor with my back against the fabric-covered speakers, listening to records over and over throughout the spring of that year, which helped me make it through my illness.

I put my journal away and reached over to turn out the light. I didn't know how much Eva liked music, but I knew she liked to dance. Maybe I would encourage Jack to play his violin for us more often. Maybe I could get a CD player for the house. Marci's friends were all raving about them. If nothing else, I could pull out all our records and make it a point to fill the house with music for Eva. For everyone.

Eva came home from work the following Monday with news of the date scheduled for her procedure. The doctors planned to do a lumpectomy and then follow up with five to seven weeks of radiation therapy. She needed to inform her employer, which she was afraid to do. As a new employee, she didn't know whether they'd keep her or let her go.

In the meantime, we talked about her convalescence here at the house and what we could do to prepare. I decided to take a couple of days off to help her get comfortable at home. Then my mother offered to check in on her during the day after that. Eva made friends easily. She already had several girlfriends who offered to help out by driving her to and from the cancer center for treatment when she was ready.

Although Eva's situation was certainly the most dire, everyone seemed to be going through their own personal issues. For example, a new problem seemed to surface in a different part of the house that week. Out of the blue Marci said to me, "Mom, Jack stinks!"

I hated to admit it, but she was right. Like some older folks, Jack would sometimes forget to bathe. When he didn't, he would begin to smell like a pot of fermented beans. Even though he had a fresh flannel shirt and khaki pants on just about every day, if you got really close to him, he definitely had a pungent body odor that needed to be addressed. Truthfully, I'd been trying to ignore the situation lately, hoping he would take to following the shower schedule I'd made especially for him. But unfortunately, that was not working out as planned.

After thinking about this for a while, trying to figure out how to really get the message across to him, I felt he'd probably deny it and make a fuss. I decided to ask Marci if she'd be willing to talk to him. I'm not sure if it was because she reminded him of his daughter or if it was a spirit connection, but she was simply the light of his eyes, and he would do anything for her. Jack always called her "Gracie" because Marci reminded him of Grace Kelly.

Marci said she understood why I'd asked her, and she bravely agreed to tackle this uncomfortable conversation. It might take a couple of days, but I knew she'd carefully choose the right time to corner him. If that didn't work, I'd have to come down hard on him and get him straightened out. We couldn't continue to live side by side with him smelling so bad.

The following week, Jack came to see me at work. While an unexpected visit from Jack was not unusual, it also usually meant a problem that needed attention. I greeted him with a kind smile, wondering, What now? But he surprised me and was actually there to officially invite me to dinner and an evening of his entertainment at 6:00 p.m. He said I could invite anyone else to join us.

I laughed and said, "Great, always nice when someone else wants to cook dinner!" Straight away, I invited my mother and told her about Jack's visit. She loved Jack and his antics and heartily agreed to attend.

I asked Eva if she was interested, but she had a date on Friday, so she passed. I loved that she was still out living life, keeping her spirits up, and meeting new people despite her recent health circumstances. Jacob had already made plans to see his wife and have dinner with her, so he passed. Margaret, of course, was leaving early Friday for the city. That left Marci, Mom, and me. Marci had planned to study but would take time to eat and listen to Jack for a while.

When I came in the back door around 5:30 p.m., the aroma was wonderful. I felt as if I were stepping into an authentic Italian kitchen—Jack's kitchen. He was a large man with more in the middle than most. With his white butcher's apron on, I could easily visualize a chef's hat on his head. Standing at the stove, stirring his sauce in a big pot, he greeted me and then promptly told me to get out of his kitchen, as dinner would be ready soon!

Since I was obviously not needed in the kitchen, I took this opportunity for some self-care. I took a shower, washed and dried my hair, then changed into sweats. I was now feeling relaxed and ready to engage with family. Sure enough, not long after, he called us all to dinner.

His gnocchi with homemade sauce was full of flavor and better than anything found at a restaurant. He also served bruschetta and a fresh green salad. After a lovely meal, we were happily entertained with more stories from his career as a theater manager working around some of the great stars of Hollywood. Finally, he finished up with a short violin concert. Whether cooking, telling a story, or playing his violin, he had a way of drawing us into his world, and he was always happy to be the center of our attention.

As Mom and I cleaned up the kitchen after our evening of entertainment, Marci asked to speak to Jack privately. They went off into the living room while we lingered, doing dishes in the kitchen. I could hear Jack every now and then raising his voice in protest, followed by quiet conversation. Well, it seems the awkward conversation about personal hygiene was happening.

Afterward, Marci explained, "Mom, he just said that he was old and forgot to do some important things, like bathing. At first, he denied he smelled. But I looked him in the eye and told him the truth. I also told him that saying he was old was just an excuse. He said he could and would do better and was very sorry if I was offended."

After that confrontation, I hardly ever noticed Jack smelling bad again. I was proud of my daughter for having a difficult conversation and telling him the truth. Hooray for my daughter and for Jack too.

Margaret returned home early Monday evening. She was a wonderful sounding board, and I enjoyed her sense of humor. I stayed up to chat with her about what was happening with Eva and her fears of losing her employment and her health insurance. Right away, Margaret had some ideas of ways to help Eva that she wanted to look into.

I slept well that evening after talking to Margaret. She had a way of being so grounding. Part of her talent was not only teaching students but counseling families. She seemed to have a clear vision of what I was creating here in our family community, at times better than me. However, she was very respectful about not making suggestions unless I asked. Having her support whenever needed was wonderful. I didn't know until a few days later that she also had her eye on Jacob. She was aware that he was struggling and that Marci was trying to help.

Many evenings, I would come home from work to find Jacob in the living room, settled into his favorite chair, reading near the fireplace. Over the years, I'd assembled quite a diverse selection of books and magazines. Everything from novels, memoirs, and mysteries to home-repair magazines and the ever-popular *National Geographic*. This bookcase collection, combined with our comfortable chairs, made for quite an inviting space to sit down for a while on any afternoon.

I began to believe that Jacob was attempting to read each and every book on those shelves. He had a real thirst for knowledge. He was also just about unbeatable at some board games. For example, when we played *Trivial Pursuit*, he'd usually win hands down! He was so sharp, had a great memory, loved trivia, and was quite adept at strategy. Still, he continued to berate himself. I think he was just stuck.

On one particular night after he skunked the pants off all of us in another one of his favorite games, Marci looked at him and said, "Jacob, you're one of the smartest guys I know. You need to go back to school."

He looked confused. "What do you mean? I can't go back to school. I'm too old, I'm not smart enough, and I don't know how to do anything but logging. Besides, even if I did get in, I couldn't afford it."

We waited patiently as he ran through his litany of excuses—a veritable parade of fear, denial, sadness, exhaustion, and unworthiness—until he eventually turned a corner. "I just never thought I had any options; it never occurred to me that I could go back to school."

Marci told him about the nearby community college, about career counselors and aptitude tests to discover different talents and professions that might be of interest to him. She told him what she knew about student loans and how a person could actually start over with a new career regardless of their age. Then she asked a powerful question that, until that day, Jacob hadn't been ready to hear. "Why not move forward?"

He sat there quietly before looking over at Marci, who was calmly waiting. She had figured him out. His stubbornness was an act to cover up his lack of confidence and direction. Eventually, he looked over at her and promised he'd go to the campus and check things out.

That night, Marci and I felt as if angels happily danced around us. We both knew that help was always nearby if we just asked for it. Maybe Jacob had been asking, and Marci, with help from above, answered with what he needed to hear.

Margaret contributed some help of her own: she had arrived home early and overheard the exchange between Marci and Jacob. So, on her way out the following morning, she left some community college brochures next to the coffee pot, where she knew Jacob would discover them. I wondered how long she had been holding on to them.

More miracles right on time!

Holidays

T HE HOLIDAYS could have been difficult for us individually. Instead, I was grateful that we were all on board to make the coming holidays really special. I intended to take them one at a time and enjoy the family participation in each.

Recently, on my lunch break, I'd been going over to the furniture store where Eva worked. While there, I could normally set aside my day-to-day life and just enjoy the experience of window shopping. I loved the smell inside the store. It was a mixture of fine leather, newly woven fabrics, furniture polish, and sometimes a distant fragrance of fresh brewed coffee. Lately, my interest included looking at dining room furniture. I hoped to buy a dining room table-and-chair set for the house. Mind you, the breakfast room was certainly a nice place to sit and eat together but kind of crowded when we were all together or if one of us had a guest. In our dining room, we had a small kitchen table and four chairs, which Jacob had found in the garage. Hanging over that old table was a lovely chandelier, which inspired me to find a more appropriate table.

One day while strolling through the store, I was surprised to find the perfect set for us. It was on sale, and I could already visualize the table and chairs coming through the front door. I wanted to buy the set, but it would have to be on credit, as I didn't have that much spare cash available. I wondered if I had enough time today to fill out any paperwork. As I made my way up the aisle to the front of the store, a salesman stopped to help me. After I explained that I was interested in buying a dining set and that I was on my lunch hour, he offered me a credit application. I quickly filled it out and handed the papers over, and five minutes later he came back and said that I had not been approved for the purchase.

Somewhat taken back, I questioned him and soon discovered that I had zero credit history. No longer a "Mrs.," I was now a divorcée and therefore suspect. Suspect of what, I had no idea. This was a huge surprise to me. I was well known in the community. I didn't understand. Was this a mistake? I was so confused. I had lived and worked in the area for years and had purchased furniture from this company in the recent past.

By the time I left the store, I was frustrated, angry, embarrassed, hurt, and a little scared. What would this mean for me? I was married when I was eighteen, and now I was forty-three. I felt I was being told that I was no longer a trustworthy shopper, that I was a high risk as a newly divorced woman, perhaps unfit to own a personal credit card. Apparently, rights for women did not include having your own credit card under just your own name. We could vote now, but we couldn't participate in our national economy by ourselves. This was hard to believe!

After dinner that evening, I talked to Eva about my frustration. As a bookkeeper, she was well aware that many companies didn't trust single women's ability to pay. She suggested I speak with the store manager and, most of all, not give up. So the very next day, I made an appointment with him. When we met, he listened as I explained why I felt I'd been denied credit. He agreed that this was likely the case and was certainly unfair. Unfortunately, this was a typical practice in the industry.

"This sure needs to change," I said.

He smiled and invited me to reapply. And so I did just that.

My application for credit was resubmitted, reviewed, and approved. As a single woman, this was the beginning of my new credit history. I was grateful that Eva had suggested I speak my mind and was also grateful to the store manager for listening to me. He took a risk with me, and I was pleased to have a card with my name on it. Without his help, I might never have been approved.

After the incident with the credit card, I wanted to be aware of what other surprises were in store for me as a newly single woman, so I talked to my attorney friend. What I discovered was interesting: The laws differed depending on where you lived. Some states were more liberal than others. What a woman could and couldn't do varied. For example, in some states, banks would allow women to have a personal savings account but not a checking account. Why? Or sometimes it was fine if you had a checking account as long as you had a "Mr." beside you doing the same. And as his "Mrs.," you could legally open a checking account, sign legal documents, open a safe-deposit box, and mutually sign a mortgage. But not on your own!

Additionally, I learned something that I thought was really strange but probably would never have discovered myself, as it was not usual for me to frequent bars: I could be refused service for spending my own money in a bar or refused the right to drink unaccompanied.

Back then—and this was the eighties, not the fifties—a woman still needed to have a father, husband, or some other male guarantor backing her. Fortunately, in the years that followed, I did find my way through the money maze within the community and had many helpful friends guide me along the path of reinventing myself—a way that felt more equitable and empowering.

In any case, thanks to my new line of credit, the new table and chairs were delivered in time for Thanksgiving. They were a nice fit in the room and looked wonderful under that beautiful chandelier. My mother, Marci, and I planned a Thanksgiving dinner at our new table and invited our housemates to join. Jacob asked if he could invite his wife, Sara. "Of course," I said, "What a good idea." We hadn't met her yet, and this was a great time to have her visit our home.

Planning this festive meal was half the fun. Mom and I prepared a shopping list of all the items we needed. Given that she made the best pies in town, I asked if she would be in charge of dessert. Her smile said yes, and soon we were on our way shopping for all the needed ingredients.

I looked forward to having Thanksgiving dinner with our created family. This time of year was about being together, building new and happy memories, and sharing our lives with one another. We were sad that Margaret couldn't be there, but she had exciting plans to visit friends in San Francisco over the long holiday weekend.

Eva had purchased a beautiful damask tablecloth with napkins to match for our dining set, so I put her in charge of the table setting. She was happy to be helping. She made individual place cards and arranged our table centerpiece with her crafting lady friends who she got together with every week. When the big day arrived, she clearly enjoyed every minute of our "oohs" and "ahhs."

On Thanksgiving morning, enough food to feed a community was being prepared in the kitchen. Dinner would consist of the traditional turkey and dressing as well as sweet potatoes, fluffy rice, green beans, pickled beets, and two salads. Jack and Jacob helped by pulling the turkey out to baste periodically throughout the day. Marci assembled a huge salad plus lots of fresh, crunchy veggies on the side with a sour cream dip. The savory fragrance of turkey baking in the oven teased us throughout the afternoon. I took care of the potatoes and gravy. Finally, dinner was upon us. It was divine! The conversations, laughter, and fun we had doing it together was what made the day extra special.

As usual, Jack took the lead, telling stories from his past. He told us all about the Hollywood stars who had shown up (or not) at his theater, about the old equipment that didn't always function properly, and of course, how he always saved the day. We all enjoyed his stories of the "good old days."

Jacob joined in and told an engaging story about his logging days—how he'd worked with a team of loggers getting a section of a mountainside cleared. He spoke about the problems and solutions in getting the job done, the balance that was needed along with the strength. He talked about the hard-to-clear places near the summit, about the equipment and transferring the logs to the trucks. He told us about the trucks that managed to drive on the very narrow roads circling the mountainside. None of us had any knowledge of how this job was done, so we were very interested in his story. You could tell that he was proud of his ability. Sara, a seemingly shy, petite woman, just smiled up at Jacob like he was something really special, which he was— he just hadn't figured that out yet! As I saw them together, I couldn't help but hope they'd be able to work things out. As soft-spoken as she seemed, I had a hunch that she had put her foot down and told him to get it together or else. Maybe this is why Jacob was here with us. And maybe Jacob was right when he said they just needed some space.

For dessert, my mother's pies were a delight. She had prepared the whipped cream topping for the pumpkin pie just before dinner. Her apple pie and her blackberry pie had just the right ratio of sweet and tartness—perfection!

I laughed and told them about my original pie-making days: I used to make and bake mud pies alongside our driveway at the home in which I grew up. I was quite well known for these pies in the neighborhood and with my family as well. I would mix the darkest earth I could find, digging from the flower beds around the house. Then I'd add just the right amount of water, using measuring cups, bowls, and pie pans I'd secretly snuck from my mother's kitchen cupboard. I fashioned my pies together, stirring mud vigorously in the bowls and pounding it into the pie pans. While the pies were set to dry on the edge of our driveway, I foraged around the yard for dandelions, blue bells, and grasses to adorn them artistically across their tops. These pies, while not edible, were spectacular.

As our conversation continued, Eva told us about several people she'd recently met who volunteered at the local animal shelter and did animal-rescue work in the surrounding towns. She talked about the urgent need for homes for some of the animals and asked if we had ever thought about having a pet. Marci and I told her about our love of animals. I talked about how, many years ago, I'd worked in a studio in California grooming poodles. Learning their specialized styles had been a creative experience for me. The grooming included bathing, drying, and clipping. Nails and careful ear-and-eye care was included. It was actually hard, time-consuming work to stand over the dogs, reassuring them while creating their look. Later, after I married, my husband and I groomed dogs in our spare time for extra income. We enjoyed this hobby-turned-income-producing project and had lots of fun taking care of our animal customers.

We also told Eva about the different critters we'd taken in and cared for in years past and let her know that we wouldn't mind helping out again. Sure enough, Eva took us up on our offer: she called from work the very next day asking if she could bring home a rescue dog for the weekend. She explained that this would give her time to call as many people as necessary to help find him a permanent home. Of course, I said yes. This is how we met a two-year-old Lhasa Apso named Clyde. He and his sister Bonnie had begun their journey on the East Coast and were now boarded at a nearby facility where they had unfortunately been abandoned. Time was up at the kennel, which meant that they were scheduled to be put down, a common practice at this time. They both urgently needed a home. One of Eva's friends took Bonnie, and Eva brought Clyde home to us.

The moment I saw Clyde, I realized he really just needed a bath. Some minor clipping here and there and some nail care would be nice too. I looked in the hall closet for my dog-grooming bag on the shelf. Then I put Clyde in the middle of my big tub. He was very good about staying put. He looked up at me with his big brown eyes and seemed to have a sense of expectant trust. I was surprised that he actually seemed relaxed and started to enjoy getting all soaped up and wet. He just stood there, patient with me as I worked over every square inch of his body, rinsing and re-rinsing the soap out of his hair.

When we were done, I wrapped him up in four big bath towels, lifted him up, and carried him to the living room where I sat down in the big rocking chair. We stayed there together for a long time. He again trustingly looked up at me and snuggled in for a nap. How could anyone have abandoned this animal? Looking deeply into his eyes, I fell in love with him right then and there. Clyde had found his forever home.

I will always be grateful to Eva for bringing home Clyde. He turned out to be quite the dandy of the household, a real character and loved by us all. He loved to be combed and fussed over every morning. He'd dance around, making sure everyone noticed that he was looking good. Soon he demonstrated his ability in the household-security department by announcing the arrival of anyone at the front door—or, for that matter, the back door. This was an important part of his family contribution. He was also a welcome distraction for Eva and played a big role in her recovery process, which was soon to follow.

Eva's surgery was scheduled for Monday morning. Like most surgeries, the morning started early. We were up and out of the house before dawn. Because the sun hadn't come up yet, the lights in and around the hospital were glowing brightly. The place was already bustling with activity. We were ushered into a small dressing-room area where Eva undressed and lay down on a gurney. She'd already gone to all the preliminary appointments required of her and was ready—as ready as you can be, given the circumstances. The surgeon had told us that a lumpectomy plus radiation was commonly called breast-conserving. Eva held her breast and said a prayer that some of it would still be a part of her body after the procedure. I echoed her prayers and felt hopeful about the outcome. Radiation would attempt to destroy any cancer cells that were left in the breast after the tumor was removed. The surgery would take anywhere from fifteen minutes to an hour. Radiation therapy would be five days a week for three to seven weeks. Some women were able to go back to work several days after surgery, while others needed seven or eight weeks before they were ready to return.

As we waited for the orderly to take Eva to the operating room, we held hands and spoke very little. I silently said the Serenity Prayer, which has always comforted me in any crisis: "God, grant me the serenity to accept the things I cannot change...." As she was wheeled out of the room, unfamiliar emotions flooded through me. I stood up, holding back tears, and moved toward the surgical waiting room. I realized I was feeling a little helpless. Without much else to do, I grabbed a cup of coffee and opened the book I'd brought.

Several other people came into the surgical waiting room as surgical procedures were getting started for the day in several of the hospital's operating theaters. More friends and loved ones were filing into the waiting room. I realized I wasn't going to be able to concentrate on my book with my mind racing, feeling too many people in the room and lots of fearful energy in the atmosphere. I walked over to the table next to the coffee machine and picked up a magazine. "Short and sweet," I said to myself. I figured I could handle a magazine with lots of pictures. Looking across the room, I could see that morning was breaking outside the windows. The sun was beginning to warm the day.

Several hours later, a nurse came in and announced my name. I glanced up, and she smiled and crossed over to sit in the chair next to me. She said very quietly that Eva was in recovery and would be there for at least an hour. Everything had gone well. She would soon be ready to go to her room. I thanked her and felt relieved for this news.

Cancer is so scary. The outcomes can vary, but it inevitably takes a toll on each person impacted. I knew that this was only the first part of the journey for Eva, and I felt grateful that we could be of help to her.

Having had the experience of waiting in surgical waiting rooms before for other friends and loved ones, I knew that now was a good time for me to take a walk, get some fresh air, and get something to eat. Hospital cafeterias are not usually the most exciting places to find delicious food, so I was delighted to find a nice selection of sandwiches, fresh fruit, and a few fresh vegetables for snacking. My choices made, I worked my way over to check out and found a table next to a big window overlooking a rose garden all trimmed out for the winter. I could imagine how lovely the roses would be in bloom come summer.

After eating lunch, some fresh air was next on my mind. Exiting the front of the hospital, I saw the familiar face of a friend from my old neighborhood.

Recognizing each other, we waved at the same time. She was here with her mother who was having some tests today. We chatted for a while then parted with promises to keep in touch. With a wave goodbye, I was off for a brisk walk around the block. I was surprised how a familiar face and friendly smile helped ease the stress I was unconsciously feeling.

Later, when I got up to Eva's room, I noticed all the equipment with the quiet beeping sounds and blinking lights surrounding her as she rested peacefully in her bed. According to the nurse, the doctor hadn't yet been by to see her. Eva had only been in her room a short time when I arrived, and she was doing well. I knew she'd sleep for a little while yet, so I busied myself with putting away and organizing her things.

Friendly nurses came and went throughout the day, checking on her, and by early evening Eva was propped up and aware of her surroundings. The doctor came by and briefed her regarding her surgery and the next steps they would take. Eva was relieved that the surgery was over and had been as successful as hoped. She was optimistic that she'd be coming home soon, perhaps even tomorrow. We both said in unison, "Thank you, God." What she needed now was rest, and I needed to go home and get some rest myself. At about that time, one of her friends arrived to take the evening companion shift.

Walking into the parking garage, I felt the cold air and smelled a hint of wet pavement. As I pulled out of the garage, I realized that the muscles in my legs and arms ached. I was still a little tense, perhaps just tired from the day of waiting and worrying. As I got to my exit on the freeway, the moist sky had already turned clear again. This was so typical of the Pacific Northwest weather in the winter months. Now the sun even made a late-afternoon appearance, reminding me that life was not all rain, doom, and gloom around here at this time of year.

Turning into our driveway, I was distracted by what looked to me like pieces of material—maybe scarves flapping in the breeze?—located at the back of the yard. I sat there in the car staring at the scene for a few minutes before I realized that these colorful pieces of fabric were actually bathing suits blowing back and forth on a clothesline. I'd never paid much attention to the old posts sticking out of the ground back there. Seeing a line strung between the posts with bathing suits hanging on it struck me as quite funny. This is the last thing one would expect to see, especially at this time of the year. Looking back, I wish I'd taken a picture of this amusing sight. A giggle started to bubble up inside of me. Of course, these suits surely must belong to our Margaret.

Margaret went to the YMCA every morning to swim laps. She spent a lot of money on her bathing suits. She'd already expounded upon the fact that if you were going to get up early every morning and swim, you ought to look good and feel great about yourself while you were at it. She would wash and freshen up her suits often, as the chlorine in the pool wore them out so quickly. Each one was a different color and a slightly different style. All were beautifully made...and did I say expensive? This day I loved seeing them refreshed and flying high on a clothesline that I hadn't known existed. Most likely, Margaret had summoned Jacob, our resident handyman, to help set up the clothesline.

Margaret, Marci, Jacob, and Jack had decided to have pizza while I was away at the hospital. Several pieces were saved for me on a plate in the middle of the kitchen counter. My housemates had been waiting for my arrival home. After changing clothes and putting on my pajamas, we all convened in the living room and visited for a while. They were curious about how things had gone, and I explained to them what I knew so far. If all went really well, she could actually be coming home the next afternoon. We wouldn't know much more until results came back from the lab.

Then, much like we shared around the dinner table every night, they each told me about their own days. Finally, we all said good night. I sure was tired. Clyde was ready to go to bed too. He jumped down from Jacob's lap and eagerly followed me to my room.

After getting home from work the following day, I was changing clothes in my room when I heard the back door open suddenly. Marci came in leading Eva's friends up the back stairs, all of them carrying bags of supplies from the hospital. I was so pleased to hear happy laughter coming from Eva's room. After getting dinner started, I went upstairs and found they'd prepared Eva's room with extra sheets, towels, and other amenities to make her comfortable during her convalescence. Soon after, Clyde's barking announced the arrival of Eva and another friend entering and slowly coming up the stairs.

Before long, Eva was propped up in bed like a frail princess with her court of three friends, Marci, and faithful Clyde gathered around her. She looked a little pale but good, with that beautiful smile and those twinkling eyes. She was so glad to be home. Her room was perfect for recovery—spacious and bright. I went downstairs to finish prepping dinner and felt very satisfied that she was tucked in bed, in her own safe healing place.

The following weeks were going to be challenging for Eva, and she was going to need lots of love, food, and rest. Luckily, we could all help out in those departments. In addition to Eva's group of good friends around her, the doctor put her in touch with counselors who'd helped previous patients and would be available to her as well. At home, Marci would be in the room right next to her with Margaret across the hall during the weeknights for added support. Margaret had told Eva about several organizations where she could get some financial help if needed. We all felt as ready as possible. We were praying for and with her.

Life is for living and hoping and caring and sharing with the people we love.
— Author Unknown

Glad Tidings and Good Cheer

J UST ONE YEAR EARLIER, Marci and I had carefully packed up all our Christmas decorations, which had been collected and enjoyed over the course of many years. We felt rather uncertain while putting them away since we weren't sure where we'd be living. Neither of us could have imagined that we'd be in this big house celebrating with these wonderful people whom, at that time, we hadn't even met. Yet here I sat, peering into these slightly dusty boxes and feeling that Christmas with our created family would be quite an experience this year for each of us.

Talking with our housemates, we all agreed that the holidays—especially Christmas and New Year celebrations—can be uncomfortable for people who are in the middle of big changes in their lives. These occasions can bring forth intense personal memories and, for some of us, even panic. All of us have stories, both pleasant and not so pleasant, about this time of year that we carry forth from our past. Creating a cozy, caring atmosphere for the season was really important to me. I wanted this for everyone else as well. Things that looked good, tasted good, smelled good, and felt good were of the highest priority to me.

Holiday celebrations could be beautiful memory-building experiences without too much emphasis on any particular faith. The music, decorations, shared meals and conversations with friends, along with the warmth and kindness expressed during this time of year, could inspire special memories to be cherished for years to come. In our household, Marci enjoyed playing traditional holiday music with her band friends who had organized a brass quintet. If they didn't have a planned gig, they would play streetside and share their music with passersby. "Joy to the world" indeed! Some days they would set up and practice downstairs, and we'd get the full "streetside" experience, except through our floorboards.

One day, in the middle of one of Marci's "concerts," Uncle Leonard called to let me know he'd be driving Michelle home from college and asked if he could join us for Christmas. I told him it would be wonderful to have him with us but explained that I was unsure of where he could sleep. "Don't worry," he said. "I'll bring my work truck with a sleeping mat in the back." Well, that solved that!

I knew that Leonard was just the right person to join all of us. He would fit right in and have great stories to tell and also be relaxed and happy to listen to others. This was important, given that we had a gifted storyteller living with us. He and Jack could take turns sharing stories about their life experiences that we'd all enjoy hearing.

Marci was excited, as she loved Uncle Leonard and we were very accustomed to seeing him during the holidays. Having him join us would certainly add a lively family member to the festivities. I wondered who else might want or need to spend the holidays with us. Perhaps a family meeting was in order, and soon.

Michelle had finished up fall quarter and was about to take a huge leap in her education and in her life: after Christmas she would leave immediately for Germany, where she would spend winter quarter doing a homestay and internship. We would enjoy having her with us, but it would be a brief stay for now.

Shortly after Leonard's phone call, Jack burst into the kitchen waving a large, curved fork, also known as a pasta claw. Since my kitchen, in his opinion, was ill equipped to properly cook spaghetti, he had to buy this essential piece of equipment before inviting me to dinner again. "Take a look at this addition, will you please," he said. "How did you ever manage to prepare pasta without a proper claw?"

"Are you inviting me to dinner or organizing my kitchen?" I asked.

"Both, now that I have the proper tools, madame," he poked back. I laughed and accepted his invitation while quickly exiting the kitchen. This would be a good opportunity to have a family meeting, and I wouldn't even have to cook dinner. Waving his new spaghetti claw high above his head, Jack marched out the door. He was certainly the spice in our life and had become not only our personal chef but also our community planner, entertainer, and dear friend.

We were fortunate that mom lived nearby and was often able to join us for dinner. She would frequently stay late and enjoy the back-and-forth conversations among us all. Recently, she'd been stopping by more often simply to check on Eva. She'd bring little treats and prepare tea. Eva wasn't ready to join us downstairs for meals yet, so when Mom came over for dinner, she'd take a tray up to her and have a cup of tea while Eva ate. Eva felt so much love from us all that she would send us little notes of gratitude back downstairs throughout her convalescence. This reminded me of an old saying that my grandmother would recite when I was a child: "Treat your family like company and your company like family." Essentially, treat one another with kindness—something I wholeheartedly believed in...and still do! My mother played a big part in my learning that valuable lesson passed down from her mother.

Jack and Jacob both complained that they could hardly get anything done because the ladies were being so noisy and disruptive. In reality, I think they were just jealous that they weren't invited to the afternoon treats-and-tea party. After they'd razzed her at dinner one evening, my mother made sure that whenever she brought treats for Eva, she brought each of them a little bag of cookies. This further established her as being the very best mom they'd ever known.

Besides being a wonderful caregiver for Eva, my mother was a good friend to me. I could share anything and everything with her. She knew my innermost hopes and fears. She could keep my secrets and help me work through any problems. As the year was coming to an end, she was glad to know I was feeling good about how life was unfolding. Her granddaughter seemed relaxed, happy, and unencumbered by any family stress. And I was making progress in building a happy life doing what came naturally to me: taking care of people and creating a healthy environment so that personal healing could take place for everyone, including me.

When Jack announced that dinner was ready, Mom came down from Eva's room to join us. We enjoyed sharing little stories, special moments, and announcements about what was going on in town, including the concerts and special events to be aware of at this time of year. I asked everyone if we could discuss our plans and desires for Christmas, and they all agreed that the time had come.

We each laid claim to doing our part to make special memories together this holiday. We agreed to not have an individual present exchange on Christmas morning. Instead, we decided that gifts of action or gifts to the whole household would be a better idea for our created family. Mom and Marci offered to prepare Christmas brunch. I offered to prepare Christmas dinner. Jacob offered to find a nice big tree for the living room. Jack offered to be in charge of a violin concert and entertainment after Christmas dinner.

I had already heard from Margaret that she was planning to stay with her daughter in the city for part of the holidays before traveling. Her spot at the table would be filled by Uncle Leonard. We decided that Uncle Leonard would gift us with his presence as our official guest. Then, shyly, Jacob spoke up and asked if Sara could be a guest as well. Everyone cheered.

Eva would be continuing her treatment through the end of the year and beyond but didn't want to be left out of the planned activities. Later that evening, while I visited her room, she suggested that Mom and she could decide on which cookie recipe to make. Eva said, "I could sit at the table and help decorate the sugar cookies." Clearly, we all felt hopeful about our holiday plans and contributions.

On the Saturday afternoon before Christmas, Michelle and Uncle Leonard arrived in his old but reliable truck. He was an artist with many years of experience who specialized in sculpting wood, stone, and metals. His truck was an important component of his business. He would haul his materials and/or finished products around to the various job sites. He'd built a large custom box on the back, which he made into storage space that served as his bedroom when needed for overnight trips. Thanks to this space, he could spontaneously drive up a mountain searching for soapstone, which he'd throw in the back—or for fun, take a drive to some hot springs halfway across the state and camp out for a few days. But right now, that space was filled with Michelle's luggage as well as the boxes and bags she'd brought home for safekeeping while she was in Germany.

After big hugs all around, Michelle headed upstairs to Marci's room with the first load, Leonard sat down in the breakfast room, and I brought him a cup of coffee. This was Leonard's first visit to see us since my divorce. I told him that Marci would be home for dinner, which he was delighted to hear. We talked for a few more minutes, and right as Michelle came back downstairs, Jacob came in from outside to introduce himself and volunteered to help.

While I prepared dinner, Jacob and Leonard unloaded the truck and helped Michelle take the rest of her things upstairs, putting some into Marci's room and some in storage under the eaves. They finished quickly, and soon we were crowded into the breakfast room for dinner. After dinner, the guys stayed at the breakfast room table, sitting and talking for hours. Once in a while I picked up a word or two, like "cedar" or "board feet." You might say they had a pot of coffee and a plate full of cookies' worth of conversation.

The next day, Jacob was already out the door before I got up. Leonard and I were on our third or fourth cup of coffee and visiting in the living room when we saw Jacob pull into the driveway with a tall tree carefully wrapped and tied down to his truck.

Leonard went outside to offer assistance. Meanwhile, I called Michelle and Marci downstairs to help me move the furniture to make room for the tree. We had the stand set up for the guys by the time they came through the front door with the tree in hand, ready to install it on the spot. Wow! What a beauty!

We took advantage of Leonard's height—at a whopping six foot seven, he was an outlier even in our tall family—and had him help us put the lights on our very tall tree. He also helped us put twinkling lights around the front porch, down the steps, and along the pathway.

Over the years of Christmas-tree decorating, the girls and I had assembled a large, multi-colored collection of ornaments—some from different countries and many hand crafted from glass, fabric, or metal. Michelle, Marci, and I spent the better part of the afternoon decorating the tree, reminiscing over each and every piece. For us, this was very much a part of our personal Christmas celebration.

When we'd finished decorating, we looked around the room with smiles on our faces. The tree was lovely. Jacob sure blessed us with his beautiful gift. Let the celebrations begin!

Mom came over for dinner that evening with Leonard, Michelle, and the rest of us. We all sat around listening to music and admiring our tree in all its glory.

For being a time of year when some people could have been quite lonely or sad, we were grateful to infuse this family Christmas with the spirit of kindness and love.

Dear Annette,

Mom, the girls, and I took time to sit down and really enjoy looking at and reading the colorful holiday greeting cards we received this year. I was reminded of a memory as a child, when Grandmother Grace lived with us. Do you remember she sold Christmas cards for extra money? And do you remember how we loved to touch the pretty velvet ones? We used to help her set up her displays. With her business-like instructions, we washed our hands very carefully. Then we opened a box, taking only one card out of the box and displaying that card on top of the box. Then on to the next and the next.

She would invite her friends over for tea to show them what was available. We liked to be nearby so we could hear them pick and choose and, well, gossip a bit too. I liked all the cards, but my favorite was of course the one with a bright red velvet Santa Claus on the front. Oh, how we were on our best behavior as Santa Claus was about to pay our house a visit.

Yesterday, Leonard arrived, bringing Michelle home for the holidays. He immediately jumped in to help with putting lights up all around the porch and creating a beautiful swag for the front door. He is a wonder! Our tree is up now too. It is so pretty, especially at night when we all sit around listening to music and admiring the ornaments collected over the years.

Eva is gaining strength and healing day by day. Clyde follows her around wherever she goes. If she is not immediately available, he finds one of us to cuddle with temporarily.

It is wonderful to have Michelle home. She leaves for Germany right after Christmas for her homestay experience there. Marci is super busy entertaining the public, playing holiday music throughout town with her friends.

This year is quite the adjustment from years past. I do feel blessed to spend it in such good company and hope to always provide a safe and loving environment for others around me. For all this and more, I rejoice!

We wish you happy holidays.

Love you more than tongue can tell,

Sharon, Michelle, and Marci

Grateful for Friendships

DURING LEONARD'S STAY WITH US, he and Jacob kept themselves busy clearing debris in the backyard. Accumulated fallen limbs from the trees out back turned into a huge pile of wood next to the backside of the garage. Off to the side of the property, they discovered and cleaned up an old picnic area, including a broken picnic table and two broken benches under some blackberry briars. By the time they finished pulling out the table and repairing the benches, the rustic picnic area looked quite inviting. While cleaning up the area, they also uncovered a fire pit, which would make good use for all that stacked wood.

Both men were accustomed to working outdoors and seemed to be enjoying themselves. When I was in the kitchen, I could hear loud shouts and bursts of laughter from time to time. A week earlier, they'd been complete strangers. Now, you couldn't tell that they hardly knew each other as they worked seamlessly side by side. Both men were generally quite shy with people they didn't know well, but today they seemed to be relaxed and having fun. Seeing the two of them together warmed my heart.

I overheard Jacob telling Leonard about Sara one afternoon—how they met, how they managed to survive the huge change in their lives (Jacob no longer working as logger), and how they both now lived so far away from their own kin. He talked about their trouble getting along and their recent separation. How nice to have a friend who seemed to be a confidant as well. I wasn't trying to eavesdrop but smiled when I heard Leonard encouraging Jacob, much like he had encouraged me throughout my life.

Eva was well into her radiation treatments now. When she wasn't resting, she would read, or sit and entertain us with stories from her life experiences. She had learned how to detach herself from her discomfort with her positive attitude. Almost always, a huge smile would greet me when I first saw her each day. I seldom knew if she was in pain, but if I asked her how she was really doing, she would tell me honestly.

I was grateful to have her home every day during this time. I treasured our growing friendship. Even though she had her own issues to deal with, she was always ready to listen, especially if I or anyone else in the house needed a friend. Sometimes her quiet presence just sitting near you was enough—a breath of reassuring air between friends.

Jack, on the other hand, seemed especially down lately. When I asked how he was doing, he confided in me that he missed his home, his wife, his life. I discovered he didn't have a close relationship with his son, about whom I knew little. He had a much better relationship with his daughter, who lived in Oregon. I would sometimes see him writing letters to them. While he was grateful to be living here with us, this was not where he envisioned himself to be at this stage in his life.

Days before Christmas, he informed me that his wife was filing for divorce. He shared with me his sadness and regret for some of the choices he'd made in past years. We talked about all the things we hadn't known and therefore couldn't change. I, too, expressed that some of my past decisions weren't in my best interest. I told Jack that I thought we were all works in progress. After sharing our hearts openly, we sat for a while with our thoughts but felt better knowing we weren't alone.

Sometimes in life a friend appears with whom you can talk about your disappointments and share your secrets and the misgivings you hold inside. You can share the sadness and shame you sometimes

119

feel. And if they are a true friend, you will not be judged. Because of this, healing often happens. I was grateful that our family community could be a vessel to foster these kinds of relationships and conversations. Over time, we all inspired healing in one another.

> *Things do not change,*
> *we change.*
> *— Henry David Thoreau*

Now on winter break, Margaret planned to visit New York City as a gift to herself. She hoped to see some shows and visit a few museums. The YMCA was conveniently located not far from the places she planned to visit. Apparently, this is where she typically stayed, or if she could afford it, she'd stay at a bed and breakfast residence hotel. Even though I would've been terrified to take a trip like this myself, I was excited for her. She promised to have dinner and spend an evening with us soon after returning to share the details of her adventures. I took this as a sign that she was extending some further trust in us. Probably because of her profession, Margaret had kept her personal life pretty close to her chest and seldom offered information about what she did, where she went, or whom she talked with. But she was now privy to some of our personal life, and I believe she felt that her experiences would be lovingly respected. As a matter of fact, a bond of mutual trust was growing within our entire family community. There were many things to be grateful for within this experiment of ours, and that feeling of trust was one of the greatest.

Maintaining my role as the mother, caregiver, organizer, and homemaker, I awoke early Christmas morning, made tea, and headed into the living room to turn the tree lights on, just like every other Christmas morning before. Sitting there quietly on the couch before the activities would begin for the day, I looked at all the ornaments from years past, some gifted, some purchased, so beautifully displayed. I enjoyed this time of reflection. I felt a moment of grace, which was the serenity for which I'd been searching. I thanked the Universe for all my blessings and truly felt at that moment the love of perfect kindness.

Just like a play about to begin, we all arrived on stage, taking our places one at a time. Leonard arrived through the back door with a cup in his hand, looking for coffee. Jacob, who had been making the coffee at the counter, laughed while filling his mug and in turn handed Jack a cup as he entered. Eva descended the stairwell with a beautiful blue afghan around her shoulders. She looked a bit frail, but her blue eyes shone brightly. Mom arrived with homemade rolls and a cranberry salad for our brunch. Finally, Michelle and Marci came downstairs. Since they were the last to arrive, we all clapped and gave them a standing ovation. They had been up half the night visiting and so took our teasing in stride, and we all laughed together. Christmas morning had begun.

Since we'd planned to not exchange gifts with one another, spending time together eating, chatting, and telling stories would be our morning. Leonard, however, had brought a few gifts that he'd made, so he shared those with us. He presented a beautifully crafted handmade chessboard for the home. Jacob immediately challenged Leonard to a game after brunch. Leonard also had several handcrafted framed collages to share with us. We all enjoyed seeing his workmanship with the careful displaying of his artful arrangements.

Eva passed around the cookies that she and Mom had recently baked. We decided that these would be our appetizers for brunch. We all shared memories of our favorite cookies from childhood. Jack, who almost always had things to say, was unusually quiet. He finally said he couldn't remember much about his childhood that was happy or fun. Jacob talked about the big snow the night before he turned ten. He was so excited to get outside to play with his sled and slide down a hill near his home that he couldn't remember eating anything. Eva remembered baking cookies with her mom, much like we did. Michelle, Marci, Mom, and I all talked about our favorite cookies, which were also on the plates before us. All these years, we were still baking the same tried-and-true recipes.

I remember admiring the tree's beauty, seeing the smiling faces, and hearing the happy laughter of our intimate group as we talked and shared stories with one another. There was an air of comfort and ease among us with some dressed in pajamas and bathrobes and some dressed for the day in jeans and sweatshirts. We were sitting around on the couch, chairs, and floor pillows, cherishing the warmth of friendship that had developed over the past few months of living together. Clyde moved from one person to the next to make sure everyone had a chance to pet him. Earlier that year, none of us could have imagined such an incredible Christmas together.

After finishing our morning with a lovely brunch, we all dispersed for a little break. We each had things we needed to do. Jacob quietly left to pick up Sara. Leonard excused himself to shower and dress for the day. Eva went upstairs and Jack downstairs for a rest.

Later we spent the afternoon visiting, playing games, trying out the new chessboard, and telling stories, and before long, it was time to sit around the table again for a dinner of delicious holiday food. After we finished eating, Jack announced that the concert would begin shortly and we should move along to the living room and take our seats. Soon he was tuning up his violin and dramatically waving his bow around in the air as we were getting settled for the show. With pillows and afghan throws around us, we were ready. Everyone there was already familiar with Jack's shtick, aside from Sara, Leonard, and Michelle, and we were anticipating that his show would happily surprise them.

Jack began playing a beautiful classical piece. But just as we began to let go and really sink into his music, he would suddenly stop playing, smile at us each individually, and state a fact or two about the piece. Then he'd tell a joke or a story until he had us all laughing, at which point he would abruptly stop talking and begin to play another piece. He certainly hadn't lost his rhythm or timing over the years—with his music or his jokes!

He beamed with pride that he had entertained us for our holiday party. This was his best performance of the year. He was understandably tired after that and sat in a chair for a long while, enjoying the conversations going on around him until he excused himself to go to bed.

A few days later, the time had come to say goodbye to Uncle Leonard, now everyone's beloved friend. We'd all enjoyed having him visit us. I was grateful that he'd gotten to experience a time in our present home and get to know the people who lived with us. He'd met some nice new people who had shared their stories with him and enjoyed his stories in return. Now Leonard was ready to move on to another adventure that was right around the corner for him. Mom came over to wish him well, and off he went, full of warm memories in his heart and a smile on his face.

This time of year often brought with it a feeling of change. And again, we were reminded of that as Marci and I drove Michelle to the airport for the flight to Germany for her new adventure. I felt excited for her and was already anticipating a letter from her in the mail.

The following week was the beginning of a new year, and after all the fun and food, like most people, I felt a little weary of the holidays. Now was a good time to put away some of the decorations and take down the tree.

At the start of the year, I always felt inspired to move the furniture around, clean, and get ready for what was to come. What would the new year bring? I didn't want or need great riches, but I was hopeful that my children would do well and that I might find even more opportunities to learn and grow. That would be very nice, and I was ready! I realized I was feeling more confident these days. I had lots of things to think about, and January was a perfect month for researching, pondering, and talking over the possibilities with loved ones.

With lots of rain, wind, and gray skies, January kept us mainly indoors. We all enjoyed snuggling down in the living room after dinner. As the days became darker, we were thankful that the lamps on the side tables gave us good light for reading.

One evening after dinner, Marci and I happened to be sitting alone in the living room when we heard Margaret pull into the driveway. She hardly ever arrived home early during her work week, which had recently resumed after the winter break. Marci and I looked at each other with curiosity. As I heard the back door open and shut, I wondered if everything was all right. Then footsteps and bags swishing back and forth as they brushed into each other could be heard in the hallway coming toward us. Margaret poked her head into the living room with a big smile on her face. "Dove Bars anyone?"

Margaret had introduced these delectable ice cream treats to us many months ago. Once again, with Margaret's support, we were reminded to set aside guilt and enjoy the simple pleasures of life. "January," she said. "A month when Dove Bars are a necessity."

"Hmm, I think you're right about that," I said. For a few minutes, I could forget about the nasty weather and just enjoy the moment. Anyone who's ever eaten a Dove Bar knows they're a classic ice cream bar on a stick. However, their decadence lies in the thick dark chocolate coating covering the outside. The surprise chocolate center was a bonus.

Ice cream in hand, Margaret sat down with us and, as promised, shared her story of going to the Big Apple for the holidays. She talked about walking the streets of the city and seeing all the colorful clothes on the colorful people. She had become quite successful as a walk-up, last-minute customer for tickets and had seen two shows on Broadway, *Sweet Charity* and *A Chorus Line*. Forgoing the YMCA, she'd decided to stay at a quaint bed and breakfast, which she said was "delicious." She'd also done some serious shopping for a few new blouses and a sweater and had brought back souvenirs for everyone, including a finely beaded coin purse for Marci and beautiful silk scarves for me and my mother. We thanked her profusely. "My pleasure," she responded.

One cold morning shortly thereafter, I was fixing breakfast for myself when Jacob came into the kitchen. He was dressed and ready to leave the house. "Good morning, Jacob," I said, "Where are you off to so very early in the morning?"

He grinned and said, "I'm going to school today."

"What?" I smiled.

He poured coffee into a thermos and then went out the door. I stood there in a daze. Month after month, conversation after conversation, Jacob had given the same repetitive response to our gentle encouragement. He'd nearly convinced me that school was not the answer for him. And now here he was, headed off to school. This truly was the first day of the rest of his life. Wow, good for you Jacob!

That night, dinnertime couldn't come soon enough. I was on pins and needles waiting to hear how his first day of school had gone. We were all present and accounted for. After setting the table, I sat down, we said our blessing, and as I passed the potatoes, I casually kicked off the conversation, trying to sound matter of fact in my eagerness, "How's it going for everyone today?"

Everyone was unusually quiet. Finally, Jacob looked at Marci and said, "I went to school today."

At first Marci didn't respond. We weren't sure if she even heard him, so he continued, "I picked up my schedule and books. I have to study after dinner."

When his words finally sank in, Marci said in disbelief, "Really?"

With a big grin on his face, Jacob said, "Yep, I'm a student now."

Marci jumped up and went around the table to give him a big hug. She congratulated him and told him to just ask any time he might need help. She was so excited for him, as we all were. He got high fives from each of us and congratulatory hugs all around, totally disrupting dinner and totally worth it.

He explained how he had talked with several counselors and looked at different pathways to a career he thought he could handle and would actually like. I could see hope on Jacob's face for the first time as he shared his experience of going to the community college campus and mingling with other students. He was surprised by how many other men and women his age were attending college. He said the campus reminded him of a walk in the forest with so many tall evergreen trees and beautiful shrubs all along the pathways to each academic section of the campus. He felt quite at home there. I was so touched to hear Jacob share his first-day experience with so much delight and enthusiasm.

What a special day this was turning out to be. An out-of-work logger finally discovers that there is life (and a new career) after logging. Suddenly, the possibilities were endless for him! This news was good for all of us to hear. As I'd learned myself, good things can happen when you risk, and for Jacob, this was a very great personal risk. Continuing to do nothing might have seemed much easier. If he took action and failed, would he handle the failure? Only time would tell, but I had a good feeling he would receive many blessings and come to rejoice in this new life he was building for himself.

Jacob wasn't the only one in the house experiencing good things. As the weeks went by, it was apparent that life was moving forward for Eva as well. She was now halfway through radiation. Soon there would be more tests and another assessment of how her treatment was progressing. During this time of rest and recuperation, she spent time thinking about her hopes for the future. She also had time to think about some past experiences that she had regrettably ignored.

One evening while we were sitting in those nice, cozy rocking chairs in her room, she was able to talk through what was going on in her head. "I've done a lot of thinking lately. I want and need to make some amends regarding leaving my husband so abruptly. And for leaving California in such a rush, for that matter. I realize now that I panicked. I quite literally ran away from the life I was living there. And I did so selfishly." She continued, "There's a little voice deep within me whispering that I need to go back to California and take care of a few things."

Eva was sorry for the pain she had caused and felt that she needed to communicate face to face with her ex-husband. She also talked about missing her children, as she hadn't seen them since moving up north. Her cancer journey was giving her a new perspective about her life and past events. I was certain that if Eva's strength continued to grow, she would follow her heart to California soon. As much as we all enjoyed her loving presence in our lives, for her, it was probably the right move. I'd be sad to see her go, but I understood her thinking and was so glad she chose to share it with me.

Life for Jack also began to take a new turn. His daughter had convinced Blanche, Jack's wife, to stop threatening him and go see a marriage counselor to be sure that filing for a divorce was what she wanted. The family attorney had also suggested this to Blanche. The counselor worked with her for a while alone, then asked her to invite Jack to the sessions. Apparently, Blanche had a lot of anger toward Jack that needed to be addressed, which seemed to surprise him. While sitting in the living room together, he told me, "I had no idea that Blanche was so angry with me for such a long period of time in our marriage." He continued to share with me, "I guess since I was gone so often, she felt abandoned. Why, it never occurred to me. Can you imagine that?"

I was touched that he trusted me enough to share his innermost thoughts. That isn't easy for any of us, and here was this seventy-eight-year-old man doing just that with someone he had met only a few months prior.

"She felt she had done her part in our marriage and I hadn't," Jack went on. "But I sent money home, I made sure we had insurance, and I paid the mortgage. I thought I did my part. I get that I wasn't much help with the kids. I hardly got to know them until I retired. Maybe by then she felt it was already too late. I don't know. She's probably right about that. I feel so bad. I never realized that I let them all down."

I shared with Jack that I had recently read how we're all spiritual beings here on earth having a human experience. We all stumble, fall, and often fail along the way in order to learn and move forward. That's why we're here. I reassured him, "Jack, there's still time to heal your relationship with Blanche. Tell her how you feel today."

I gave him a big hug and a smile. My deepest desire was for Jack and Blanche to work out their problems and reconcile their relationship. How many years did they have left here on earth? I felt such deep empathy and compassion for both of them. Making a marriage work can be very challenging. And sometimes, no matter how hard we try, it still falls apart. As he left the room, he picked up his big blue book and headed for his bedroom.

One day as I headed to work, I could smell snow and feel the moisture on my cheeks. The gray skies and gloomy clouds continued to hang around throughout the day. In the early evening, snow began to fall like thin scraps of paper coming down. A strong wind blew in from the north, and the snow seemed to be angled straight toward the house. Hopefully the storm would be mild and over soon.

As it happened, we ended up with a few days of snow followed by several days of melting. I made a big pot of stew and biscuits for dinner the first night—a proper meal for a snowed-in kind of day. After dinner, I wrapped up in a warm blanket with a good book and our guard-dog-turned-lapdog, Clyde.

While sitting near me in the library with his own book, Jacob assured me, "I'll get up early tomorrow morning and take care to clear the walkways and the path out to our cars, too."

"Thank you, Jacob, I really appreciate you!" I said, smiling up at him from my chair.

As he headed out of the room he said, "You're welcome, ma'am. Just doing my job."

From our front window, I watched neighbors helping one another remove snow from walkways. While winter brought a lot of gloominess with its weather, it was a great reminder of the kindness and support that surrounded us all. I loved the community-minded people in this town and how it always seemed that a helping hand was there when needed. This was true within our intimate home community as well.

Rejoice

Changes Are Coming

S EVERAL WEEKS LATER, I received a surprise phone call from Germany. I recognized Michelle's voice right away, which brought a huge smile to my face. She had great news for us: she had finished her work-study program and homestay experience and would be on her way home soon to stay with us for a week before heading back to college.

That evening, I shared with Marci the news of Michelle's call. How could winter quarter already be over? We were both excited about her coming home and happy that she'd be able to stay with us a bit before going back to the campus for spring quarter.

Soon, the time came for us to pick up Michelle from the airport—bags, boxes, and baggage in tow. We talked and laughed all the way home. Being together again was so wonderful. As we pulled into the driveway, Michelle took in the view of home and told us how much she'd enjoyed the holidays with us and how comforted she felt while gone to know that her things were set aside in her own little storage area upstairs. Straightaway, she had a nice visit and cup of tea with Eva and Mom, who had just arrived. When Michelle followed Marci upstairs to get settled in, Eva told me how lovely she thought the girls were. They were so like one another. Of course, how could I argue with that? I totally agreed!

Jacob spent the day studying in the dining room for an upcoming test while Jack took over the kitchen. Jack delighted us all with his favorite lasagna casserole and a salad for dinner in celebration of Michelle's arrival. I was again grateful for his help, as I'd been busy picking her up at the airport. Michelle was thrilled to have pasta for dinner. She told Jack that his lasagna was the best she'd ever had. He beamed at having pleased her for her first meal back home.

During dinner together, Mom and I could see that Michelle wanted to share stories of her experiences in Germany, which we were excited to hear more about, but she was starting to fall asleep at the table. The flight had been very long. Tired from her trip and ready to relax, she excused herself to shower and rest.

Saturday, we all gathered in the breakfast room in the morning for coffee and a typical German breakfast and to hear all about Michelle's experience. It all started with the aroma of rich black coffee followed by plates of cheese, salami, crusted rolls, fresh unsalted butter, and soft-boiled eggs sitting up individually in little holders with small spoons to scoop out the eggs. There were lots of questions and answers back and forth as to how to eat the egg without breaking or spilling it before getting it into our mouths. We ate well and listened intently, spending all morning laughing and enjoying ourselves greatly.

Later, Mom and I were having tea while the girls were upstairs. Hearing them laugh and talk like the children at play we remembered from long ago was so wonderful. They didn't leave us alone for long before they came bounding down the stairs, giggling and appearing through the doors of the dining room. Michelle was carrying a box that she carefully set down on the table before she went to pour tea for Marci and herself. Was this a little surprise? Removing the lid from the box and lifting out a wrapped bundle, she explained that while she'd been abroad she'd wanted to find a treasure to help her remember the trip—something of personal meaning to bring home. Carefully unfolding the bundle, we saw a small hand-carved black walnut cuckoo clock in the shape of a birdhouse. The tiny door at the peak of the house would swing open, revealing an enchanting little blue bird that sat on the ledge and announced the hourly time. It was really charming, and the workmanship was exquisite.

Her handcrafted surprise came from the Black Forest, which is famous for its carved cuckoo clocks, produced in the region since the 1700s. The area, located in the southwestern part of the country bordering France, is also known for its dense evergreen forests and small, quaint villages that are often associated with the Brothers Grimm fairy tales.

Over tea, Michelle told us even more about her homestay experience. She'd become quite fond of her homestay family, which consisted of Mother, Father, one son no longer living at home, and one going to high school. She said that being with a family and completely immersing herself in the German language was very good for her. Having an internship at a local radio station, she enjoyed new experiences daily. She also learned about the city of Cologne and talked about casually walking by the famous Cathedral Church of Saint Peter each day on her way to work. Can you imagine?

She seemed to have a new sense of confidence. Listening to her, I realized that I'd played an important part as her mother, giving her the roots to grow and wings to fly. I gave thanks to the

Universe for taking such good care of her while she was so far away.

Within a short time, she would report to the International Department of her college, where a new chapter would begin as she accepted a part-time job as a coordinator working on campus with the incoming international students. Like many other students, Michelle continually faced the stress of time and money, but at least this job would provide some much-needed income for her while she was completing her final quarters.

Just as Michelle was moving forward, so were we in our own life experiences. I knew that change was just around the corner for Marci and me.

One evening, I was having tea with Eva after dinner. As usual, we were sitting in the rockers, facing each other with afghan throws around our legs. She smiled and said, "Did I ever tell you about that night out when I didn't come home until the sun was coming up?"

I giggled. "No, but I was hoping you eventually would. All I remember is you told us you were going downtown after work to meet friends for dinner."

"Well, yes, that was the plan, but while I was with friends at a local restaurant, I was introduced to a very handsome man. It turned out that he also loved to dance, so it seemed right to go hopping from one club to the next with him. We also sat and watched others dancing. We laughed and agreed that people-watching was fun. We ended the evening by walking the pathway along the waterfront, talking and sharing about each other's lives. I secretly was feeling so ugly and unworthy. I thought I'd never have an evening out like this ever again, let alone an evening with the personal attention of any man."

Eva smiled as she continued to reflect on the evening. "He was generous in so many ways: his listening, his compliments, his encouragement at just the right times. He shared that he'd been going through a personal transition himself, and he seemed to be enjoying my company as well. We'll probably never see each other again, but it was wonderful. You know, sometimes with a stranger you let your hair down, relax, and just let yourself be honestly and totally present."

Somehow, with reminiscing about her magical evening, I saw that Eva had a renewed sense of self. She seemed to have a direction in mind. That sentiment was reinforced when she revealed that she'd contacted her son in California. I knew they had a good relationship. He'd invited her to come and stay with him for a while, and she'd decided to take him up on the offer. She'd given notice at the furniture store, giving them a generous amount of time, as they'd been so good to her this past year.

They were sure to miss her warm smile and sunny disposition. And now she was reluctantly giving me notice as well.

We'd all had loving and memorable times with Eva. Marci and I were sad to see her planning to leave but happy for her at the same time. We trusted her judgment and knew she'd continue to find her way. Later, Jack suggested we throw a going-away party, which Eva warmly welcomed.

"What a good way to not only say goodbye to my friends but also a great way to have one last party with everyone," she said. We agreed. Next month would be a good time for the celebration.

Mom dropped by the office around noon the next day. She had a handful of daffodils that were freshly picked and ready to open up to the world, a slender vase, and a cute card with a big sun shining brightly on the front. She knew that every year I looked forward to crocuses, primroses, daffodils, and then colorful tulips in abundance. I placed the card and flowers on my desk for personal inspiration and joy for all. We still had some gray and rainy days before we'd consistently enjoy the sunshine. These daffodils were sure to bring a little brightness into our lives in the meantime.

Beauty is such a simple thing: a
tender bud, a bird on wing
— Author Unknown

With a now dear friend leaving and a room becoming vacant soon, I realized I needed to put another ad in the paper. In addition, I intended to have a talk with Margaret when she got home, as I would need all the help I could get to find a new housemate to join us. I loved our family community, but our ability to stay in this house depended on having each bedroom occupied with a person willing to help us with a shared expense.

When Margaret arrived home that evening, I was able to catch her before she retired to her room. I told her of Eva's plan and the vacancy upstairs starting the middle of next month. She gave me a wink and some reassurances that she'd snoop around on campus and see if anyone was looking for a place. Knowing this was Margaret's home away from home, I felt confident that anyone she might suggest would be great.

Jack was excited to be in charge of the going-away party. He felt this way about any party, for that matter, as he loved to be creative. Playing the social director of the household also offered him a nice distraction from his own circumstances, which often found him confused and sad. When Mom came for tea and a visit, Jack asked to see her alone. They convened to the living room to discuss party plans. She loved Eva as much as the rest of us and was thrilled to help Jack with the planning.

While the two sat together, fully immersed in party planning, I peered out the kitchen window and was happy to see little flowers popping up all over the place, bringing a smile to my face. Jacob, ready to be of service again, was out in the garage, tending to the lawn mower, making sure it was ready for the rounds of mowing that would soon be required. I admired his dedication and how he was thinking ahead.

Actually, I'd noticed that Jacob had a whole different air about him lately. When he made the decision to go to school, his entire mindset and demeanor changed. I felt he was a happier man these days. He'd become quite organized with his time and was committed to setting aside time for his wife as well, which I thought was truly sweet. Since they'd been living apart, I could see that they had reinvigorated their relationship by first reestablishing their friendship and then allowing each other a chance to grow in their own personal way.

Sara had a job working at a large garden center near their trailer park. She shared with me how she had always loved plants and thought she would fit in nicely at the center. This was her first time working outside the home. At first she was terrified, but soon she began to feel more confident. I heard from Jacob that Sara was a loyal employee and a hard worker, arriving early every day. She loved seeing the flowers arrive, sometimes already blooming in all their glory. She fussed over and cared for the plants and flowers as they began to adjust to their new environment.

As Eva prepared for her move, I still hadn't received a response from the ad placed in the newspaper. I was wondering when or if we'd find our new addition to the household. I was beginning to feel a little anxious about our household expenses. Not even Margaret had anyone in mind. We all had a growing awareness that our family was about to go through a big change. As the saying goes, the only thing that's inevitable is change! Each of us had become quite familiar with that truth in our lives.

Several days later, Marci came to me and asked if I'd consider having a student come to live with us for a short period of time. She knew a student looking for a place to stay. I hadn't thought of that possibility. My original thinking was to make housing available for people who were in transition, such as when a person's marriage ends or folks who were new to the area.

She said, "I think you'd like this girl and would want to help her. She needs to find a calm, safe place to live so she can finish high school. She plans to go into the military after she graduates. She says her grandmother will help her with any expenses."

"Okay," I said. "Let's see what this is about. Perhaps she can give us some background as to what's going on in her life right now and how we might be of some help."

The very next day, Marci brought Mikaela home from school. We didn't approach the topic of her possibly moving in with us then, as we had a party to take care of first. It turned out that she loved to plan parties and was a big help getting things ready and blended right in with the family.

Mom and Jack did a phenomenal job with all the planning, preparing, and decorating, and even with the invitations. Surprisingly, having had little to do with the planning made the party a lot more fun for me.

It was delightful to receive all the welcoming smiles and handshakes from friends and also from many people we didn't even know. Then there was Eva. She was full of her typical upbeat energy. She would sleep well tonight, I was sure. Her time with us in the last few weeks showed us that she was almost back to normal. We met her friends from work, church, and hobby and craft clubs, and from her evenings of dancing. Along with the delicious food and festive decorations, I discovered that our home was a perfect venue to have lots of people flowing in and out of the common areas. Eva had a very nice send-off from her family community around her with special thanks to Jack and Mom in the planning and preparation department.

A cheerful heart
and smiling face
pour sunshine
in the darkest place.
— Author Unknown

Sunday afternoon we finally got the time to sit down alone with Mikaela in the living room. I loved that time of day as the sun was pouring in through our front windows. Clyde was curled up on Marci's lap. Jacob, with a book tucked under his arm, casually left the room. Mikaela sat in the rocking chair, quietly rocking back and forth. After a few moments of silence, she began to share her feelings. "I...feel kind of trapped at home. My stepdad and I don't really get along much. When Mom's at work,

I'm left alone with him. We argue. I have a hard time concentrating on my schoolwork. I don't feel safe there with him. I've been thinking of just leaving. My mother doesn't seem to understand. She'd like me to stay right there because I'm the one who actually takes care of my younger brother and sister's needs. But I just can't anymore."

She tipped her head down for a few moments, as though in deep thought. Then she looked up at me and continued with her story. "We recently got into this big fight. My stepdad thought I should do more around the house. I felt I had been doing lots of things and told him so, but he just kept ranting and raving. Pretty soon, in a rage, he just hauled off and hit me. I landed on one of the potted plants, and dirt went everywhere. He demanded that I clean this up immediately. There was no way I was going to do that. When I told my mother what happened, she took his side. She decided it was time for me to leave, as it was hurting her relationship with him." With a bemused smile, Mikaela shook her head. "I was surprised. Leaving sounded great, as far as I was concerned, but where? How was I going to find a place to live?"

I was really angry and sad to think her mother would choose her man over her daughter. I wondered what was really going on there. It was very clear to me that staying there would be dangerous for her.

Mikaela's grandmother wanted to help but lived too far away. Mikaela couldn't stay there and go back and forth to school. She was very close to graduating; she just needed to finish out her last year of high school, then she could move on with her life.

But did we have what she really needed? Would we be enough? Both Marci and I shared with her what we'd been creating here, a place we could all call home. We gave her a brief description of who lived here with us and the house rules we were all living by. I needed to talk to her mother and her grandmother before making any kind of decision. I asked Mikaela if she'd be okay with that idea, and she said yes.

After dinner that evening, Marci and I gathered in Eva's room for one last heart-to-heart visit. Eva took my hands in hers and said, "Sharon, you were there for me when I needed it most, and I will always be grateful for your help and support." Tears welled in our eyes.

I smiled and said, "Eva, thank you, and let me say to you that the support went both ways."

"Eva," Marci added with a nod of emphasis, "as the self-declared house cookie-supplier and the one responsible for all the deliciousness, we are clearly going to be in trouble. Whatever will we do without you?" We all laughed, passing cookies and tea around as we enjoyed our final moments with one another.

A short while later, Jacob yelled up the stairs, "Eva, are you ready?" He wanted to help her maneuver a few pieces of her acquired furniture into the little trailer she'd rented for the move. He had a morning exam to study for and would be gone early.

Eva left home while I was at work the next morning. Jack and my mom stood on the porch and waved goodbye. This was just as well, as I would've had a hard time holding back tears as she drove away. As it was, her departure was still very emotional for me. I found myself tearing up most of the day and from time to time in the days that followed. Eva was the first to come live with us, and now the first to leave. I knew this was life moving forward, but saying goodbye was nonetheless distressing for me. I felt a level of fear again. I thought, "So strange, when my faith is tested, I forget to trust in the goodness around me."

I went upstairs to sit in Eva's light and sunny room, allowing some memories of her time with us to flow. Ahh, her sweet gift of the little flowers that started our African violet collection sitting on the kitchen ledge overlooking the backyard. Eva was also the one to introduce game night in the household, which we all loved and cherished. Her stay with us had been filled with tons of laughter and silliness. I loved how she'd taken on the role of house cookie-baker and how during the holidays, even when she wasn't very strong yet after her surgery, she and Mom had prepared the Christmas cookies. In addition, Eva just had that special something about her that projected warmth and love. She demonstrated an extraordinary ability to listen with no judgment.

As I rocked in one of the chairs she loved to sit in, I thanked the Universe for bringing this woman into our lives. She taught us about love, patience, and kindness. While I may not know exactly how, I know that the time spent with Eva over the past year was life changing for us, and we were all the better for having known her. Though the time she spent here offered challenges with her health, she grew stronger in her sense of self. In this loving and supportive place, she made some important decisions about her future. As she would be remembered fondly by each of us, I imagined she would remember her experience of growth here for the rest of her life too.

Still rocking gently in the chair, my mind shifted to the question weighing heavily on me now: should I accept Mikaela into the fold of our family community? This would be her first time away from home, and I wondered whether she was ready to venture out into the world on her own. Equally, I understood the need for her to have a stable environment in which to live and study as she finished out her schooling.

I thought about how we could give her a place where she could feel safe, have some peace and quiet to study, and gain more clarity about her life. I felt the piece of paper with the phone numbers of Mikaela's mother and grandmother in my pocket. And I placed the call.

The conversation with her mother was uncomfortably brief. She said it was okay for her to stay with us and that I might want to talk with her grandmother, as she was going to pay Mikaela's shared expenses. That was about all she had to say.

Talking with her grandmother, I actually discovered she didn't have a lot of insight into Mikaela's present home life either but knew she needed to be in a family-like environment where she felt safe. She said I could count on her for financial support with supplies, clothing, and expenses incurred while she lived with us.

Speaking with Marci again while she was settled in her room for the night, I asked if she felt sure about Mikaela coming to live with us. As ever, Marci was inspiring to me as she explained that this was the right place at the right time for Mikaela, that we could be a part of her much-needed stability and help her on the way to the rest of her life. I went to sleep that night feeling pretty confident.

The next morning, I called Mikaela and shared the news of a room available to her. She seemed immensely pleased. That very day after school, her mother brought her by. She signed the house rules page and paid her shared expense before going up to her room to take a look around.

Spot Cleaning

THE FIRST THING I DISCOVERED about Mikaela was that she apparently loved shoes and clothes— mainly shoes, of which she had quite a few. I also discovered that she'd done a lot of babysitting to afford those shoes. She brought some pillows and a bedspread that she liked better than the one that was there. She worked hard at transforming her room into her space and style, pounding nails into the wall for her pictures and decorations. I could see that doing this helped her feel a sense of ownership over her room. Upon arriving home, Marci welcomed Mikaela with a wave as she went by her room. I had a good feeling that Marci and she would become good friends. Soon she'd develop a trust in all of us, I hoped. She needed to know that we really cared about her.

At dinnertime, Jack and Jacob were careful not to scare her with their stories (which were sometimes exaggerated) or their loud voices arguing back and forth over who knew something better. To my surprise, Mikaela actually seemed quite happy, relaxed, and not at all afraid. She jumped right in, helping Marci do the dishes after dinner—a nice bonus for Marci, who sometimes got left with that task mostly by herself. I heard them giggling and banging around while I was off doing something else in the house. Then up the stairs they both went to study.

When I got home from work the next day, I found Mikaela in the kitchen standing by the sink, wringing her hands furiously as if drying them in midair. Smiling, I said, "Hi, Mikaela, what's going on?"

She looked at me with a worried expression and said, "Please, may I clean and organize the cupboard under the kitchen sink?"

"Okay," I said slowly. "Goodness knows that the space under the kitchen sink could always use a little help. Would that make you happy right now?"

She quickly answered, "Yes, yes. I just need to straighten things out a bit, tidy things up a bit." In my mind I saw her shoes perfectly lined up in her closet. Order! She needed and wanted order.

Looking into her troubled eyes, I said, "Mikaela, if that's what makes you happy, you are now and forevermore in charge of all things under the sink."

I gave her a big hug and left the room to change clothes before coming back to make dinner.

I decided not to overthink or be disturbed by Mikaela's behavior. While she was with us, I never questioned why the cleaning products were sometimes all over the counter when I got home after work. But within a half hour, all was straightened out and in good order under the sink, and Mikaela was back upstairs studying with Clyde on her lap. Like each of us, he was doing his part in helping her mend and feel at home.

As the days progressed, she seemed pretty well adjusted, considering the trauma she'd experienced in her previous home. Though I didn't feel the need to delve into the details of her story, I was so glad her mother allowed her to leave that situation. I actually felt that her mother was happy not to have to worry about her anymore. I knew that Mikaela was in counseling, where she could get the help she needed. I sensed that my job was to provide consistent kindness and a home where love was present. She reminded me of a lost kitten that had found a place to rest awhile. She was a little skittish and emotionally frazzled, in need of all the love, kindness, and patience we could produce. My hope was that we could give her a good start to a calmer way of life.

Margaret was also good for the girls at this time in their lives. She had such a charming way of showing love and respect to her fellow housemates. I knew that counseling young adults was part of her job and was grateful to see her in action in our own home. Marci and Mikaela were often up late studying, so when Margaret would arrive home from work, she'd sometimes surprise them with a little treat, like those divine Dove Bars. The giggles and quiet laughter could be heard all the way downstairs. The three of them had established an unspoken bond.

Margaret would also show me her love and respect in so many sweet ways. She enjoyed flowers, as I did, and would often leave a new specimen of some different or exotic flowering plant for me on the breakfast room table. I would be so touched to see this in the morning before heading out the door to work. While she was often not present at dinner or our little family parties or gatherings, she was very much present in our lives in small but equally valued ways.

The following Sunday at dinner, I noticed that Jack was not his usual entertaining self, and I wondered if he was feeling all right. While Marci and Mikaela were busy in the kitchen cleaning up, I cornered him in the living room and asked if he was okay. He looked down at his book and then at his shoes before responding, "Life is complicated."

I agreed. Life *is* complicated! Giving him a big hug, we both let out a little sigh. As we sat down, he continued, "Marriage counseling is really challenging." I asked him what he'd like to see take place during this therapy. With his eyes still cast down to the floor, he replied, "Oh, I don't know; I just want to go home and for us to live in peace."

I was happy he was in counseling. It seemed to be helping him and, from what he shared, Blanche too. Neither seemed particularly happy or comfortable with the way their life was going right now. One thing he shared about his wife was how she admitted to the counselor and to Jack that she had an anger problem. She also admitted that she'd stretched the truth about what Jack took from the house, passing the blame onto him for things she couldn't find or remember where she'd placed. I was happy to hear this, as it sounded like they were getting somewhere and beginning to repair things through their honesty with one another. The counselor indicated to them that it was never too late to work on their marriage. Jack repeated this to me several times.

I sincerely hoped that Jack and Blanche could find some peace between them. He'd certainly come a long way from the Jack we first met. At first,

I was a little concerned about him, especially when seeing his frustration play out over little things. Now he was much calmer, a better listener, and better able to accept some of the things in his life that he couldn't change.

The next evening, Jacob's wife, Sara, joined us for dinner. We were beginning to see her more often now. Sometimes she'd join me for a little walk in the yard, talking about life in general and some girl talk too. There was a bush that Mom and I had been speculating about for weeks. At this time of the year, it was in full bloom with cascading tendrils flowing down its side, and we were hoping Sara could help us identify it.

Sara recognized it in an instant: "Oh, what a beautiful weigela!" Happily satisfying my curiosity, she went on to say, "Weigelas used to be very popular many years ago and only recently have been making a comeback." I was pleased to hear that Sara was enjoying her job, as she deserved to be doing something she loved and felt competent in doing. Finding out about new plants was her favorite part. I thanked her and knew that from now on she was going to be our go-to resource regarding whatever was planted in the yard.

Sara knew our backyard well. Whenever she came for a visit, she and Jacob would spend time together outside and would often take long walks back beyond the trees. So today was our turn to walk to the property line, where she showed me the immense base of the poplar trees and, just in front of them, the bamboo. For some time, Jacob had been telling us about the clump of bamboo, which was at least fourteen feet high, mingled among the poplar trees.

As we made our way back to the house, Jacob was standing at the edge of the bamboo forest waiting for us with a serene expression. He always seemed happier outside. Sara walked up to him and timidly took his hand as they walked around the side of the house and out of sight. I smiled as I watched them walk away. Things seemed to be going nicely for them as well, together and individually.

I was in the kitchen making tea the next morning when Jacob came in to fill his coffee thermos. He'd been leaving around seven in the morning and returning home around three in the afternoon. He was a fully immersed, full-time student now, carrying a B+ average, which was so exciting. Marci and I had become his cheering squad.

Much like his wife, Jacob had a love for all things growing. Plants were his ongoing hobby away from school. This benefited our house tremendously, as he planted hyacinths, tulips, and daffodils, which involved planning and playing with the bulbs back in February. First, he went to garage sales and found containers to place them in and then put them all over the house with careful thought as to the proper amount of sunlight. Before long, all of them were blooming in the living room, dining room, and kitchen. There were spectacular combinations of red, yellow, orange, pink, and lavender.

Soon we realized we were living in a greenhouse. With Sara's help, he began to plant other little specimens using more containers collected on his rounds of garage sales. What a joy to watch him and see what he discovered along the way! Thanks to him and his newfound interests, we all enjoyed a variety of plants that were lovely shades of green, some with delicate flowers, and a few of which had the most wonderfully sweet fragrances. Seeing him so invigorated and excited was inspiring and fun for all of us.

The next couple of weeks turned out to be pretty emotional for Mikaela. She either appeared very happy and quite talkative or was extremely depressed and stayed in her room. Nearly every day, I wondered if she'd make it to school or not. Finally, at dinner one evening, she told us, "My plan was to go into the military when I finished high school. But I recently found out there's a long waiting list. I may be qualified and even enlist but can't actually depart for about a year after I graduate. I'm pretty bummed, as I don't know where I can live after I graduate or how I can support myself while waiting. I know that I absolutely cannot go back to my mom's place."

We all had questions and thoughts, things that we could say but didn't. We each acknowledged that her news was distressing and would take some time to figure out. I could sense by what was not being said that the rest of us were all grateful to leave the dinner table and move on with the evening since there was nothing that could be said or done right now. For this troubled teen, feelings of disappointment were heavy. My prayer over the coming days was that time would reveal more about life to her and that she'd discover what to do next. In the meantime, I assured her privately that she had a place to live until she was ready to move on. She seemed relieved but still troubled about her future not moving forward exactly as planned.

Several weeks later, Margaret invited my mother, Marci, Mikaela, and me to visit her home in the city on a Sunday afternoon. She explained that this excluded Jacob and Jack, as it was to be a "girls' day." She would often say, "One day I'll treat you to brunch at my house." Given that she was quite mysterious about where she lived and usually unavailable on the weekends, this invitation was as unexpected as it was delightful. All four of us were curious and giddy about the excursion.

Sunday arrived with the moist Northwest morning dew on the grass. We jumped into the car and headed for Seattle. Destination: Margaret's house. How refreshing not to worry about the normal weekday traffic or have a time schedule for any of us.

She lived in an older section of the city near a large park. After many years of decline in property values, the area was becoming quite popular again. Young people were moving back into the neighborhoods, which were actually very near the downtown core. Leaving the freeway and driving almost immediately into this district, we could see giant madrona trees growing along some of the city streets. There were also beautiful old evergreen trees planted here and there.

We turned a corner and approached a steep hillside. Looking up, we noticed Margaret waiting on her porch doorstep waving a yellow bandana so that we could see which house was hers. As I climbed my way up the stairs to the porch, I wondered how many more years she'd want to make this climb. Being up among all the trees and branches, it felt like she lived in a birdhouse.

Inside, I noticed the beautifully waxed wooden floors and cheery setting of both the living and dining room, which apparently, she hardly ever used. She explained that she spent her time in the kitchen and upstairs, where her bedroom and bath were located, along with several other bedrooms, one of which she used as her private office.

After touring the house and quaint yard behind it, we came back in and sat around the kitchen table. She had prepared a lovely lunch, which included shrimp-stuffed avocado, rolls, and fresh greens with a light oil and vinegar dressing. Fresh sliced strawberries and whipped cream topped it all off.

While we ate, she explained that she'd begun working on upgrading the house many years ago: improving the roof, plumbing, painting, and installing new floors and a glass cubed wall separating the bath from the shower, among other renovations. Little by little, projects were completed. Only a few more years and she'd retire. This house was a part of her retirement plan. She would sell it, possibly to some young couple who didn't mind the climb up those formidable front stairs. We all had a good laugh about that. Her plan was to purchase a small condo downtown near the market, theaters, shopping, and, of course, the YMCA pool. It seemed like a good plan for her—one that matched her values of self-care and quality.

We had a lovely afternoon together, which I would cherish for a long time. Margaret had become an extension of our family, and we hoped her dreams of retirement and living in the city would come true.

In the back of my mind, I got to thinking about the house we lived in. Surely this house was an investment for Mr. and Mrs. Van. No doubt they'd had similar conversations about the future of their home. I knew that originally, they'd lived in this house with their children for a while. I wondered how their children entered into the future of the house, if at all.

As if reading my mind, Mr. Van called that following week to let me know that his grandsons and he would be out to finally finish repairing the remaining windows. First thing Saturday morning, they pulled into the driveway in a bright red Ford pickup. One young man was sitting in the back of the truck and the other men were inside up front.

We exchanged greetings, and Mr. Van asked to have a rundown again on which windows still needed repair or replacement. We walked around the house as I pointed them out to him. He thanked me, and soon they all got busy. I'd forewarned everyone that this project was going to happen, as I figured it would involve lots of banging and moving in and out, which it certainly did.

The next morning was quite the opposite: a quiet calm in the house. Very little action from any of us. I did a little reading with a library book in hand and snuggles from Clyde. Mom dropped by and had tea with me. Having tea together quite often was satisfyingly normal for us. If we didn't see each other every day, we at least spoke on the phone. Meanwhile, Mikaela had gone to visit her grandmother. She'd left to catch a bus very early and had told me it would be a long day and not to expect her home for dinner.

Marci and Jacob spent the day studying. Jack had slept in again this morning, but now he was in the kitchen preparing his amazing sauce. He announced that we would forever remember him by his incredible sauce. Of course, Jack said something like this each time he took over in the kitchen. I just smiled and left the area, glad that he was stirring the pot.

Another Goodbye

I N RECENT WEEKS, I'd noticed that Jack was
sleeping in longer every morning. When he first
started living with us, he'd be up very early and I'd
find him reading in the library area before I headed
to work. But now when I'd go home for lunch, he'd
just be getting started with his day—making his
breakfast of decaf coffee and a piece of rye toast just
about the time I'd step in the back door. I wondered
what had caused the change. I knew he and Blanche
had been going to counseling now for several
months and that it was helping Jack, but of course,
I wasn't privy to Blanche's experience. Jack had also
gone to his doctor for a checkup and yearly tests
recently. Perhaps more would be revealed to me
soon, and I knew I had to trust and just let go. This
old man had certainly wormed his way into my heart.
Was I now being overly concerned about his
sleeping habits?

The following Monday afternoon, Jack stopped by the office. He seemed upset, so we stepped outside to talk for a few minutes. I said, "Jack, what's going on?"

With a furrowed brow, wringing his hands, he said quietly, "You might say I'm a little troubled. As you know, I spent the day with my daughter on Saturday. She drove up to see both her mother and me. Apparently, she'd been talking with Mother about our little situation." Jack continued speaking almost in a whisper and with a kind of confused look on his face. "Well, she said Blanche is ready for me to come home." Jack looked at me and asked, "Am I ready to go home?"

With deep care and concern in my heart for this elderly entertainer whom I had come to love so dearly, I said, "Jack, the first thing I suggest you do is talk to your counselor. See what he has to say and then ask yourself, 'What's best for me today?'" He gave me a big hug, sighed, and walked away mumbling to himself. I stood there a few minutes, smiling and with tears in my eyes. I couldn't help but feel his mindful confusion. He was such a sweetheart.

With it being close to the end of the school year, every night there was some event to attend or something to prepare for the following day.

Suddenly having two girls rather than one made a difference in the number of activities. We could barely keep up with the pace. I was really looking forward to the weekend to serve as a bit of a breather for us all.

Friday finally arrived. Somehow this seemed to be a Jack dinner night recently. This week, he planned to prepare his favorite spaghetti dinner for those of us who'd be home. Marci and Mikaela came home with their friend Brad and hoped he could join us for dinner, which delighted Jack to no end. He was pleased to share and, of course, brag about the meal he was about to serve. Brad had known Mikaela since she arrived at their school and had become a close friend over the past few months. Marci knew him from the band, and the three of them made a great trio of fun and laughter, with each one outdoing the other with pranks or jokes. Being the organizer, Jack got along with them swimmingly and put them to work right away making a big salad while he made the sauce and supervised the stirring.

Because I'd gotten off work early that day, I decided to hang around the kitchen to watch and learn how the master actually made his now-famous sauce. Jack had created this many times, but I knew that each batch tasted a little different and was always completed with a lot of love and attention.

He said, "My secret is in the tomatoes, the freshest ripe tomatoes I can find. I start with a handful of garlic cloves, a little oil, onions, then the tomatoes, a seasoning pouch full of oregano, basil, and a few crushed red peppers. I add some tomato paste and water, then simmer all afternoon. If I have it, I throw in a crust of Parmesan cheese rind for extra flavor."

Pacing around the kitchen, he'd keep a close eye on his sauce, occasionally stirring and dramatically waving his pasta fork around. His sauce never disappointed. The actual amounts of ingredients were subject to his mood and how large a batch he wanted to make.

Jack also thought that his pasta preparation was unique and the very best. He said, "First boil the pasta until it's al dente, then give it a light rinse and drain. Slip the noodles into a very large bowl. Add two large soup ladles full of sauce to the pasta. Be gentle and blend this in so each noodle is well covered with its own jacket of specialty sauce."

He boasted, "My noodles will not stick to each other, and they will be blush pink in color, sitting in the center of your plate or pasta bowl." Then he'd put a heaping ladle of his magnificent sauce on top and often add a meatball or two on the side.

We all thought this was perfection!

Jacob had invited Sara to join us, but she had other plans to go to a house party with a friend. Still, there was no way Jacob was going to miss out on Jack's sauce. As usual, Margaret would be in the city, so the only person left to invite was Mom. Just as this thought entered my mind, she came through the back door with a pie in hand. Without any planning, this evening was turning into an "end of the year" family dinner party. Sometimes the best things in life are unplanned and unexpected.

The next morning, I sat in the living room, reading the paper and drinking my tea with Clyde by my side. I was surprised to see Jack come up the stairs so early. He made his coffee and joined me. He said, "I think I am ready to go home now." My heart sank hearing those words, as I so enjoyed having this old man around our home. We sat together for a while, helping each other get comfortable with this new realization. I asked him if he wouldn't mind bringing me up to date regarding the counseling process and the counselor's thoughts about them. He felt that the sessions over the past few months had been very productive. He and Blanche were no longer blaming and pointing fingers at each other. They'd even had a few chuckles back and forth over past behavior on both of their parts. Maybe enough healing had taken place and the time had come. Jack laughed. "I used to have the confidence of a fool. Now I'm not even sure what I'm thinking or feeling half the time."

I reminded him, "Maybe Blanche is also struggling with her thoughts and feelings. I'm sure you're not alone in this."

"Yeah, you're probably right," Jack said. "We have been in each other's pocket for a very long time. Even though we're having a little problem communicating right now, I believe Blanche is ready for me to come home. And I think maybe I'm ready to go back."

Even though I'd been anticipating this, I was surprised at how sad I felt. I didn't expect to get so attached to Jack. His energy was magical! Who knew that this man, who I'd been quite unsure about welcoming into our home, would turn out to be such a great housemate and a fun entertainer, loved by us all? His dumb jokes, lively music, and aromatic dinners would be very much missed in our home. Mom would miss him too, as they'd had so much fun creating parties and figuring out what food to serve. Jack gave and received a lot of love here and had become such an integral part of our home community. Like everyone else who came to live with us, he had become family. I most certainly wanted what was best for him, but I sure would miss him. We all would.

In truth, we all wanted Jack to be happy and to rejoice in a "reunion of spirit" with his wife. I wasn't sure how difficult or easy it would be for them, but I was proud that they were willing to give it their best shot. Jack assured me that he felt they needed to continue with counseling. I was surprised and grateful to hear those words from him. They'd been married a long time, and this was like starting over in some ways. It's pretty incredible how we never know what twists and turns are around the corner and where life will take us.

Dear Annette,

Mikaela is staying with us now. Her personality is so bright and full of expectant wonder. We have her in the room Eva was in. She very quickly made it her own (books, boxes, bags, and shoes). She is Marci's age and also about to finish up her schooling here. Her plans are to enter the military soon.

Senior prom was a huge success for both the girls. I made Marci's dress, which was pretty and pink. Mikaela's grandmother made hers, which was a beautiful blue. Both girls looked lovely, and they both had a fun evening. The group had lots of photos taken. I knew they were having dinner before the dance at Shoreline, always a great place to dine. Later they told me that they only stayed at the dance for a while and then went to Denny's for fries and Dr. Pepper. Can you just imagine?! I thought it was pretty special that Marci had actually known two of the guys since kindergarten and one of the gals since first grade. They are about to begin a new kind of school, and I wonder if they will continue to know each other.

Now I'm saying goodbye to another dear member of our family here. First Eva and now with Jack preparing to leave. I rejoice for all that I have been gifted. Since moving into this home, I've learned that I'm capable of mothering and caring for people while enjoying life and gaining a renewed inner confidence in myself. What I will do for myself in the future, I'm not yet sure. But I'm open to the possibilities that may be given to me and, in the meantime, thank the Universe for each and every one of these folks in my life.

Love you more than tongue can tell,
Sharon

Summer Days Ahead

WITH SCHOOL NOW OFFICIALLY OVER and both girls graduated, it was time for Marci to head out to a weeklong band camp. Many students would be moving on to colleges that had large music programs or, more specifically, marching bands, which they all agreed were 100% the best. She was really looking forward to breaking out and having some fun, playing music, and just being with friends.

Meanwhile, Mikaela found a job at a daycare facility within walking distance of the house. But first she was staying with her grandmother for a week before starting her new job.

Margaret, after finishing up the end-of-year paperwork on Friday, left for Hawaii. She certainly knew how to have fun and live her dreams! I still had a lot to learn from this woman.

Jacob had a little break before starting summer classes and had convinced Sara to leave for a weekend in Portland, Oregon, to visit relatives and enjoy the beautiful Pacific Northwest coastline.

As for Jack, he decided to spend the weekend with Blanche just to be absolutely sure, leaving Clyde and me at home. Wow! What a strange feeling, to be completely alone in the house, a first since moving here. The walls and my heart still felt the presence of friends and loved ones, so although I was definitely alone, I didn't feel lonely.

On Saturday morning, I did household chores and shopping for the following week and then wandered through the house with Clyde following me around. I felt a bit restless having only myself to take care of. I imagine he picked up on that and was hoping I'd settle down so he could curl up and take a little snooze on my lap. Eventually, he got his wish as I sat on the couch and read my book. The sun was now pouring through the front windows, making everything nice and cozy for us, and I ended up falling asleep as well.

As I slowly woke up, I enjoyed some peace and quiet with myself to reflect upon the past amazing year and think about what was next. Michelle had recently told me that the father of the family she'd lived with in Germany felt it would be good for his younger son, Klaus, to experience family life in another country. Klaus's father wanted so much for him to have an American experience before he headed off to college and was hopeful Michelle knew someone he could stay with. She asked me if we could help him make this dream come true and house him. She even proposed that she room with Marci for the time he was here to help out since she'd be on summer break.

I had thought her idea was an intriguing one and would be a great experience for all of us, but how could it work? Where would we put him? We didn't have an extra room available at the time; otherwise, that would have been a natural solution. I assured her I'd keep my ears and eyes open and see if something made itself known. And so it did—with Jack's thinking that the time had come to go home.

After enjoying a simple dinner by myself, I curled up on the couch with Clyde once more and called Michelle to tell her about Jack's decision to move back home. She was really happy for Jack and Blanche but must have heard the sadness in my voice. She offered me comfort by saying, "I know you'll miss him. He's been like the spice in the sauce of your home!"

I laughed. "Things certainly won't feel as lively around here—or smell as yummy," I said.

She chuckled and then eagerly asked, "So does this mean there's room for Klaus?"

"Well, yes, I guess it does!" I said, smiling into the phone. "Isn't life interesting? Just when you aren't sure what to do next or how something will work out, life offers you the solution." Klaus might very well have a nice homestay experience after all.

When Jacob and Sara returned from their little getaway, we had tea and cookies and I heard all about their trip. Both of them were all smiles, and I wondered if he would be leaving soon too. How could I complain though? Watching Jacob grow was another gift for my soul. I was so happy that they seemed to be working things out and finding happiness once again. Happiness for Jacob was discovering there was life after logging. For Sara, new happiness seemed to come through her job and doing what she loved.

Marci returned from camp and was greeted by some changes in our home situation. I made her favorite chicken soup dinner with biscuits and took some upstairs to her room. She told me about her nice visit with Jack earlier in the day and how he'd told her about his weekend with Blanche. "He said they didn't argue all weekend and that he'd made the decision for sure to go home and was feeling happy and confident again. He even had a grocery list in his hand and was already planning meals for them." She shook her head and added, "I wish he could stay, but I know it's the right move for him. It's like you always say: accept the things we cannot change, right?"

We both sensed that we'd be seeing him from time to time and were very happy for them both, even if it would be quieter around the house without him. I told Marci about my conversation with Michelle, to which she replied, "I guess it's time to move on. It'll be fun to meet Klaus and have Michelle at home with us for a month as a bonus." I smiled at her optimistic attitude. We both were adjusting quite well to the changes taking place in our lives now.

That Saturday morning, Mr. Van returned with his grandsons for yet another round of maintenance to fill several holes that had formed in the driveway and to repair two front steps that had recently become loose. It seemed as though the house and property were suddenly receiving a lot of attention these days. Was it because the weather was so nice? He also repaired the leaky faucet in the kitchen sink, which had been bugging me for a while. With Jacob having been so busy the past few months with school and rebuilding his relationship with Sara, we hadn't had the same amount of help around the house with fixing things that fell apart. I appreciated all this help from Mr. Van. He did say when we moved in that he'd take care of any repairs, but he hadn't been consistent. I was happy he was finally getting around to it.

Michelle put together a schedule of planned activities and events for Klaus, keeping in mind that most of us, including Mikaela, would be working. That left Michelle and Marci to do the "showing around." We looked forward to meeting him. I was pretty sure he would become a new friend of the family, just like all who had come and stayed before him.

Over dinner, we told Jacob more about our soon-to-be houseguest. He was also getting used to meeting different people by now. I laughed and told him that we were just broadening his horizons. I was also excited for Klaus to meet my mom and Mikaela. Margaret would be back from her trip before he would need to return home, so he'd get to meet her too. This was our family community, an important part of life now, and I wanted Klaus to meet them all if possible.

During the following week, I was delighted when I bumped into Jack at the grocery store while doing the weekly shopping. He was in the vegetable aisle squeezing some tomatoes when I came up behind him and tapped him on the shoulder. Caught mid-squeeze, he turned around with a guilty look on his face. When he saw it was me, he sighed with great relief. He laughed and gave me a big hug. No surprise, he was selecting tomatoes for his famous sauce. Catching up with him in the produce aisle, I told him about Klaus coming to visit us, and he promised to come over, join us for dinner, and meet the lad.

I also brought him up to date about Eva, who'd called several nights earlier to tell me that she'd arrived safely at her son's despite getting a flat tire and running out of gas. What an adventure! The plan was for her to stay there a few months to get her bearings. She also had a date scheduled with her ex-husband for dinner and conversation at their favorite restaurant. More would be revealed later on about how that would turn out, but I hoped she was prepared for any outcome. Making amends, let alone some sort of reconciliation, isn't always easy. Jack nodded in agreement. I knew he understood about working things out better than most.

The heart that loves
is always young.
— *Greek Proverb*

My First International Student

S EVERAL WEEKS LATER, Marci, Michelle, and I met Klaus in the baggage claim area of the airport. He was a tall, blond, handsome young man with blue eyes and a little dimple in his cheek. Both girls were also tall, which made them a great-looking trio of young people walking down the corridor together.

Fortunately, English is required for students in Germany, so Klaus could understand us. Because of his accent, however, I couldn't always understand him. So, I was about to have my first experience communicating with a non-native speaker. I felt pretty comfortable as long as I was concentrating and looking directly at him.

By the time we got home and settled in with a snack of tea and freshly baked apple pie, Klaus was already falling asleep, so we bid him *gute nacht* and left him to a long-awaited night of rest.

Within days, we discovered just how much Klaus loved our big house. It was a pretty typical Northwest-style home, yet to him it seemed exotic. He took countless pictures of it for the memory book he was creating. We planned to take it easy with him the first week, given the jet lag and new surroundings. We just took small outings—driving around in the afternoons to show him the town, the college campus not far from the house, the park, and the nearby river and bicycle walk. We had beautiful weather during his stay, so Klaus could see the magnificent mountains that surrounded our town, which were breathtaking this time of year.

One day, Michelle and Marci took Klaus to Snoqualmie Falls so he could see and experience the spectacular waterfall. He was soaking up the beautiful scenery this part of our world had to offer. After their excursion, Mom, Jacob, Mikaela, and I joined them for dinner at our favorite seafood restaurant, located near the Shilshole Bay Marina. They were known to serve incredible Pacific salmon dinners. While we enjoyed our meal, Klaus told us about his home and the town where he was born. Jacob asked him about the surrounding area where he was raised, and Klaus couldn't stop talking. Where he lived was simply magical according to

Klaus. They laughed heartily. Both were very inquisitive and not afraid to ask lots of questions. We ladies just sat back, listened, and were entertained by their curiosity.

The next morning, it was time to decide what else Klaus would see while here and to create a plan to visit some memorable areas. The kids sat down with a notepad, pencil, and map of the Northwest. They would definitely do the Seattle Pike Place Market, Seattle Center, Space Needle, and Hiram M. Chittenden Locks, originally opened by the U.S. Army Corps of Engineers in 1916. Given that Klaus was an engineering student, Mikaela thought he might find that interesting. There was also a great fish ladder there to observe the return of migrating salmon.

During lunch, while attempting to assemble a hot dog for himself, Klaus managed to artistically squirt bright yellow mustard all over both the hot dog and the front of his white shirt. Shocked by what had just happened, he stood there frozen with a mustard bottle still in hand. We all burst out laughing. What a mess he was! This turned out to be a famous memory in later years simply because of his shocked expression. (I might add that mustard is very stubborn and does not completely come out of fabric no matter what you use or how hard you try to make it happen.) Right on cue, Jack came up the back steps and into the kitchen. He must have enjoyed catching us with our expressions of surprise, along with poor Klaus standing there dumbfounded with the bottle and hot dog in hand. We all shared another hearty laugh. Jack stayed for lunch and, after Klaus had cleaned up, Jack asked him all about his life and family in Germany. Of course, Jack then took us all on a journey with his words, as he could do so well, telling us stories that had Klaus in stitches.

On Friday night, the girls took Klaus to his first drive-in movie. We had a great drive-in theater in the Valley with several good flicks playing. On Saturday, there was a local sidewalk sale in the downtown section of town, along with a classic car club show. Jacob offered to take Klaus, who was beyond excited. Klaus loved classic cars made in the US, especially any that he recognized from movies. The cars were parked at an angle down the center of the main street so people could see how beautifully restored they were. He was sure he had just arrived in heaven. Apparently, according to Jacob, he stopped and talked with nearly every owner of every car on the street. This was such a memory-building day for this young man.

The following week, Michelle and Marci took Klaus to Seattle. Klaus asked to go shopping downtown to look for a pair of red Levi's jeans. This eighteen-year-old had a fascination with not only old cars but red jeans as well. It was vital that he return to Germany with a pair for himself as well as his friend. Evidently, Levi's were a sensation there within his circle of friends at school. Marci said they shopped all afternoon specifically for these jeans. They went to five department stores and some side shops—looking, asking, pleading for red Levi's. Both girls got pretty exasperated with him after hours of hunting.

While in a boutique on Fifth Avenue, they had him buy a replacement for his mustard-stained shirt, which sadly would never be the same. But unfortunately, he arrived home without the sought-after jeans. I guess they weren't as popular here as in Germany.

The girls were thoroughly enjoying their time with their new international friend. They had quickly established as comfortable a rapport with Klaus as if he were really their brother. This meant they could (and sometimes did) argue like siblings as well. All four were quite opinionated and felt strongly about different issues. I happily stayed out of the way.

Mikaela had to work, but the other three planned to take off on Monday morning for Vancouver, Canada. I had no idea what they planned to see or do there, but it surely would be a fun little road trip

191

for them. Having grown up several hours away by car from the Canadian border, Michelle and Marci were accustomed to visiting Canada once or twice a year. This time would be especially fun, taking a friend who was excited to see new areas. They would be gone for the week. I have to admit, having four young adults in the house who were boisterous, happily laughing, and just "all in" over everything could get pretty noisy. I knew Mikaela would miss it, but for me, the quiet was most welcomed.

Shortly after I returned home from work Monday afternoon, Mr. Van arrived—this time with just one of his grandsons, Sam, who we'd gotten to know fairly well during this past year. They wanted to have a talk, so I invited them in and made some coffee. I had leftover brownies in the cupboard that I knew Sam would enjoy. As we sat down, my mother came through the back door and up the stairs into the kitchen. Feeling right at home, she proceeded to fix herself a cup of tea and join us at the table.

Mr. Van smiled and began to reminisce about the years he'd lived in the house, how much he and his wife and children had enjoyed living here, how they had updated the furnace and plumbing and made other home improvements. He said, "I'm so happy you've also shared my enjoyment of this house." The way he was talking, it felt like he was leading up to something. As if he could read my thoughts, Sam patted his grandfather's arm and sighed softly.

Now I knew that this was not another casual visit. Mr. Van proceeded, confirming my suspicions, "My wife and I have decided to sell the house. I didn't want to at first, but she convinced me that it was time. I know she's right, but still...I wanted you to know as soon as the decision was made. It will go on the market within thirty days."

He knew I would need time to find another place, and I knew there were other people to consider as well. He continued reminiscing about his children and the house for another half hour. I tried to be polite and attentive, but my stomach was churning. I was not expecting or ready for this new development and was just trying to assimilate the information and not panic about everything that needed to happen so quickly. I looked over to my mother, who had always been my support system. She gave me a loving and reassuring smile. From the start, I knew that the "project" would have to come to an end one day. I suppose I was simply caught off guard that it was actually happening now.

Mom stayed for what felt like a somber dinner. I shared the news with Jacob, and he told me right away not to worry about him. He said he could go back to living with Sara, as things had been improving between them now for quite some time. He also assured me that he'd be available to help in any capacity to get my things moved to a new location. What a great friend he had become, one of many gifts received this past year.

I figured Margaret would need some time to get things in her life organized before school reconvened, so getting in touch with her was a priority for tomorrow. When I called to break the news, she must have picked up on my concern. She said, "Okay, Sharon. Stop and breathe." At first, I was confused and didn't understand why she was saying that so firmly. She continued, "There's no need to worry. We have lots of time to brainstorm about this during the week."

As I hung up the phone, I took a deep breath, remembering what I'd learned and practiced this past year: change the things I can and accept those things I can't. Of course, this kind of change, a decision to move, is much easier if it's your own choice. While I knew from the start that living here was only temporary, I had become quite comfortable in this house. Now I felt nauseated and out of breath.

I spent the day feeling so many emotions, reminding myself throughout to stop and pay attention to my breathing. Something as simple as that made such a difference as I sat with this new reality. Thank you, Margaret, for reminding me to stop and breathe.

Sending out a few prayers to the Universe for guidance, I took some time to reminisce about the past year and the people I'd welcomed into this home. Each person was a gift to me. Thanks to Margaret, I learned to take better care of myself. This actually occurred naturally by observing Margaret taking care of herself and doing so with such joy.

Then I thought about Eva and realized how she taught me a deeper level of acceptance. Watching her remain optimistic throughout her cancer diagnosis and treatment was quite moving and inspiring. She also modeled how to listen and trust herself. Her decision to go back to California, while a surprise to me, seemed to be just the right action for her to take.

Watching Jacob blossom into a happy person with direction and a new lease on life was thrilling. I believe that this occurred because of the loving patience and encouragement we all afforded him. Equally, he gifted me with the reminder that it is never too late to start over.

And then there was Jack Daniels, everyone's favorite entertainer and chef. He taught me how to live one day at a time. He reminded me that it's okay to laugh a little more, relax, and allow myself to be supported by others. Both Jacob and Jack showed the courage to change the things they personally could. Because of their determination, their lives were completely changed for the better.

Having Mikaela come to live with us was also a special gift. She became very much like our very own. I'd begun to think of her as my "bonus daughter." She was such a treasure.

I guess it's fair to say that our "project" was a success. We managed to afford living in a big old beautiful house in downtown Claremont, which was our initial desire. This house took care of our needs. It was always there to welcome us home from our various outings. Each room held important memories, much laughter, and a few tears. We had some hellos and goodbyes and were encouraged to grow emotionally as well. Perhaps most importantly, this home offered each of us a safe place during a transition while we prepared for what would come next.

By the end of the day, I was feeling a calm sense of acceptance and completion. I didn't have a solution as to where we might live, but I knew we'd be okay and that we'd welcome this new phase of our life just like we had before. I believed that our angels were lining up to help out wherever needed.

The next day, Mikaela came home from work and Klaus and the girls arrived several hours later, tired and happy but glad to be home. After they got settled, we all gathered around the kitchen table, and I shared the news about my visit with Mr. Van. At first, they were surprised but then seemed actually excited for me. They spent quite a while giving me loving advice about what to do next. Each person had some good ideas for my future. This was so sweet. I went to bed that night feeling relaxed, loved, and full of a few new ideas myself.

Several days later, while driving Klaus to the airport to see him off to Germany, Marci turned and asked Klaus what he would remember most about his trip to America. He looked out the window, and then turned toward the girls with a smile. In a most respectful way, he said, "I shall always remember that you are my American family, my home when I come to America."

This would not be the last time I heard something very similar from someone who came from far away to live with us for a while.

A New Beginning

B Y THE END OF THE SUMMER, Marci, Mikaela, and I had moved into a small house near our local college. Settling into a new place to call home, I cherished the memory of the people who had filled my world with love, laughter, and the kindness of community living.

Shortly after moving, I became aware of and intrigued by the possibility of becoming a host mother, providing a homestay experience for international college students. Michelle, working in the international department of her college, suggested this, as she knew there was a great need for host families. So I called our nearby college and offered to help. I was confident that my desire and openness to this was a direct result of the experience we'd just been through.

My hosting experience began the following year and would last for another ten years. Once all three of my girls were living away from home, I found great pleasure in opening my home to international students who needed a place to call home while they were here studying.

During my time as a host mother, I had the pleasure of housing and fussing over more than a dozen young adults from several different countries. I learned so much about how families were structured in their countries. I learned about what their day-to-day lives were like, their special holidays, and sometimes their belief systems. I enjoyed their companionship and loved getting to meet several of their mothers on their first visits to America.

One thing that became very clear was how being away from home was quite challenging for the students. It required a lot of discipline. Sometimes afraid, yet persistent and brave, they kept moving forward step by step with their education. Some acquired two- and some four-year degrees while here, and some just came for a quarter of school and the American experience. My students called me their "American Mother," a title I wore happily.

I was grateful and surprised at how well prepared I was to support them through their transition. I had gained a lot of knowledge in the year of our "project"—having a shared-expense community and being a homemaker, caregiver, friend, and mother to all. But perhaps most importantly of all, I found personal happiness in living one day at a time. And it all began in a place we called home.

Epilogue

WHAT HAPPENED TO EVERYONE after this experience? Many housemates kept in touch, and I was able to get updates on their "post-project" lives:

Eva did enjoy family in California but then moved to Texas to be near her daughter and spent many years happily readjusted there. Cancer returned with a vengeance, and she has now transitioned.

Margaret did retire. She sold her house in the trees and ended up happily residing in the city, as she had hoped.

Jacob finished his degree and landed a wonderful job in the aviation industry.

Jack and I kept in close contact. His wife seemed relatively satisfied to have him back home and was happy that he was once again cooking for them. He transitioned a little over five years after living with us, and she followed him several years later.

After working locally for a year, Mikaela was finally given an enlistment date. She spent time in the Air Force, learning a trade and serving in Germany. She's back in the Pacific Northwest and now has two beautiful children and a granddaughter.

Klaus finished his education, became an engineer, and is now married and living happily in Germany.

My mother, their "G-ma," lived for many years after the project, either near me or with me, and has since transitioned.

Marci went on to college and studied abroad in Japan, which sparked a lifelong love of that country. She and her husband, Akira, live in Tokyo, where she is a writer.

Michelle graduated, worked for her university, and then began her career within the airline industry. She and her husband, George, live in Michigan.

I am now retired and living happily with Michelle and George.

Clyde spent his remaining years as our Sergeant of Arms until it was his time to cross over the Rainbow Bridge.

Acknowledgements

THANK YOU TO MY FAMILY for being both helpful and patient with me while I wrote this book.

Thank you to my beta readers, cover designer, and photographer.

Thank you to my accountability partner, technical advisor, and daughter, Marci Kobayashi.

Thank you to my daughter Michelle Mufarreh, who encouraged me and helped me rethink and rewrite many pages along the way.

Thank you to my son-in-law George for being my in-house tech and print master.

Thank you to Jodi and Dan, who have been inspirational mentors and assisted me with the book's creation all along the way.

Thank you to Amanda Johnson for guiding me in my initial stage of writing.

Thank you to Olivia, my Boston terrier, for listening to every word I read out loud.

Thank you to the people of our created family community in *A Place Called Home*, without whom this book would not exist.

About the Author

S HARON SMITH was born in the Pacific Northwest, where she spent the majority of her life. In addition to hosting international students in her home, she owned a uniform business for healthcare professionals for many years in her community. She has a daughter and son-in-law in Japan and a daughter and son-in-law in Michigan, plus a bonus daughter in Washington State.

After retirement, Sharon moved to Japan to live with her daughter, Marci. While there, she began writing her blog, *Sharon's Walkabout* (sharongracesmith.com), which led to her writing this memoir. She now resides with her daughter Michelle and her family in Dearborn Heights, Michigan.

She is a contributing author in *Goodness Abounds: 365 True Stories of Loving Kindness.*

Made in the USA
Middletown, DE
29 July 2023

35925948R00119